CULTURES OF THE WORLD
Ghana

Patricia Levy and Winnie Wong

ᴍᴄ **Marshall Cavendish**
Benchmark
New York

PICTURE CREDITS

Cover: © Sune Wendelboe/The Image Bank/Getty Images
alt.type/Reuters: 33, 38, 41, 68, 71 • Bes Stock: 13, 15, 32, 34, 35, 36, 44, 45, 48, 49, 72, 74, 76, 82, 86, 120, 122, 131 • Corbis Inc.: 39, 40, 54, 55, 69, 85, 106, 108, 109, 111, 113, 114, 128, 130 • Getty Images: 21, 43, 52, 57, 58, 80, 87, 92, 96, 98, 101, 103, 105, 107, 116, 126 • Hutchison Library: 14, 62, 95, 102, 119 • Lonely Planet Images: 7, 61, 83, 89, 115, 127 • North Wind Picture Archives: 22, 24, 26, 27 • Photolibrary: 1, 3, 5, 6, 8, 9, 10, 11, 12, 16, 17, 18, 19, 20, 23, 25, 28, 30, 31, 37, 42, 46, 47, 50, 53, 56, 59, 60, 63, 64, 67, 70, 79, 81, 88, 91, 93, 94, 100, 112, 117, 118, 121, 123, 124, 125, 129 • Topfoto: 75 • Trip Photographic Library: 65, 66, 104

PRECEDING PAGE

A man and boy rowing among reeds on the calm Volta River in Ghana.

Publisher (U.S.): Michelle Bisson
Editors: Deborah Grahame, Mindy Pang
Copyreader: Daphne Hougham
Designers: Nancy Sabato, Lock Hong Liang
Cover picture researcher: Connie Gardner
Picture researcher: Thomas Khoo

Marshall Cavendish Benchmark
99 White Plains Road
Tarrytown, NY 10591
Website: www.marshallcavendish.us

© Times Media Private Limited 1999
© Marshall Cavendish International (Asia) Private Limited 2010
® "Cultures of the World" is a registered trademark of Times Publishing Limited.

Originated and designed by Times Media Private Limited
An imprint of Marshall Cavendish International (Asia) Private Limited
A member of Times Publishing Limited

Marshall Cavendish is a trademark of Times Publishing Limited.

All Internet sites were correct and accurate at the time of printing. All monetary figures in this publication are in U.S. dollars.

Library of Congress Cataloging-in-Publication Data
Levy, Patricia, 1951–
  Ghana / Patricia Levy and Winnie Wong. — 2nd ed.
     p. cm. — (Cultures of the world)
  Includes bibliographical references and index.
  Summary: "Provides comprehensive information on the geography, history,
    wildlife, governmental structure, economy, cultural diversity, peoples,
    religion, and culture of Ghana"—Provided by publisher.
  ISBN 978-0-7614-4847-1
  1. Ghana—Juvenile literature. I. Wong, Winnie. II. Title.
  DT510.L48 2010
  966.7—dc22   2009023139

Printed in China
7 6 5 4 3 2 1

CONTENTS

INTRODUCTION

THE WEST AFRICAN REPUBLIC OF GHANA was named the Gold Coast when it was a British colony, as it possesses one of the world's largest reserves of gold. The many European forts that dot Ghana's coastline attest to a past where foreign traders settled in the once-great Ashanti Empire, seeking its gold, ivory, and slaves. A significant number of Europeans were employed as advisers and administrators. Ghana learned how to govern itself and became the first modern African country to retrieve its independence. It takes its name from a kingdom that once flourished to the north of the modern state. With its vast natural resources, a peaceful political climate, and premium education for its people, Ghana is set to become a leading African nation in the 21st century.

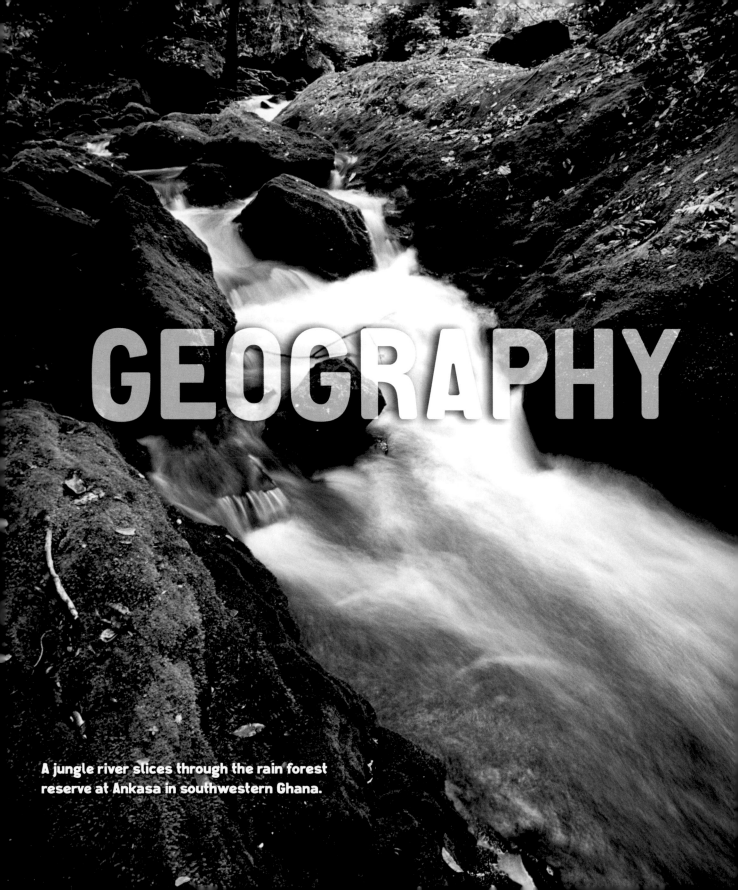

GEOGRAPHY

A jungle river slices through the rain forest reserve at Ankasa in southwestern Ghana.

CHAPTER 1

GHANA IS LOCATED IN WEST AFRICA, 400 miles (644 kilometers) north of the equator, on the Gulf of Guinea, which forms 420 miles (676 km) of its coastal southern border. To the north lies Burkina Faso, to the west is Côte d'Ivoire (Ivory Coast), and to the east is Togo. With a total land area of 89,166 square miles (230,940 square km), Ghana is slightly smaller than the American State of Oregon.

Ancient metamorphic rock formations dating back to when Ghana was still part of Gondwanaland can be seen today in the Accra Plains and the southern part of the Volta region.

The beautiful Biriwa Beach in Ghana lies between Cape Coast and Saltpound.

About 4.5 billion years ago Ghana was part of a supercontinent called Gondwanaland, made up of present-day South America, Africa, India, and Australia. Some 600 million years ago the land sank, creating a huge interior lake within Ghana. The Mesozoic era, 220 million years ago, saw the breakup of the supercontinent and the creation of the separate continent of Africa. Later still, around 70 million years ago, the land surface was forced upward, forming the modern topography of Ghana. Ghana consists of four regions—the coastal plain, the forest-dissected plateau, the savanna high plains, and the sandstone basin of the Volta region.

TOPOGRAPHY

THE COASTAL PLAIN This long, low strip of sandy shore is intersected by several rivers and streams, most of which are navigable only by canoe. It stretches 50 miles (80 km) inland at its eastern and western ends, but narrows to around 10 miles (16 km) in the middle. Divided in half by the capital city of Accra, the coastal plain is low lying, with an average elevation of 246 feet (75 meters) above sea level. Some areas, such as the lagoon at Kéta, are below sea level and occasionally flood.

An unspoiled palm-fringed beach on the tropical coast near the mouth of the Ankobra River.

THE FOREST-DISSECTED PLATEAU The plateau occupies a large triangular area of the southwest of Ghana, including part of the southern coast. The landscape is mostly gently rolling hills, with broad, flat valleys in between. The region consists of primary rain forest in the extreme southwest, with plantations of hardwood and cacao trees, which produce cocoa beans, making up the rest of the plateau.

Elephants and savanna-like vegetation dominate the landscape of Mole National Park in northwestern Ghana.

THE SAVANNA HIGH PLAINS This inverted L-shaped band of land in the north and northwest of the country varies from 300 to 2,900 feet (91 to 884 m) above sea level and is made up of smoothly undulating plains dotted with occasional small, rounded hills.

The land is dry and covered with tall grasses, some reaching 10 to 12 feet (3 to 3.7 m), low bushes, and the random tree. Because of the underlying rock that blocks draining, some parts are swampy. From November to March no rain falls in this region, and the land dries out completely. Nevertheless, the plants survive as they have adapted to withstand long periods of drought.

A view from the topmost point in Ghana, Mount Afadjato, part of the Akwapim-Togo mountain range.

THE VOLTAIAN SANDSTONE BASIN This consists of about 43,540 square miles (112,770 square km) of land in the eastern half of the country. Like the northwest, it is covered in savanna-like vegetation, but is low-lying and flatter, at some 200 to 600 feet (60 to 180 m) above sea level. Around its edges rise several ridges and mountains.

To the east is the Akwapim-togo range, which includes Mount Afadjato at 2,903 feet (885 m), Ghana's highest point, while to the west is a long, narrow plateau. At its heart is the water system of Lake Volta.

CLIMATE

Although close to the equator, Ghana has a moderate climate with sunshine throughout the year. The southwest is hot and humid, while the east is warm and dry. In the north temperatures during the dry season can reach 100°F (38°C). Nowhere in Ghana do average temperatures fall below 77°F (25°C). The hottest time of the year in the south usually is April, just before the long wet season. The coldest is August, just after the wet season. All of Ghana experiences dry and wet seasons, but the effect of the dry season is less noticeable in the south. The coastal area and the forested areas have two wet seasons—a long season between April and July and a shorter one from September to November. The north experiences only one wet season, between September and November.

THE HARMATTAN

The harmattan is a wind that affects large areas of Africa. It originates in the Sahara and blows down across Ghana from the north and northeast. It is a hot, dry wind and carries a large amount of red dust, which is deposited throughout the country. The forested areas in the southwest of the country break up this wind and protect the southwest from its drying affect.

The harmattan can be devastating. In 1983 it blew across the entire country, disrupting the rainy season and causing a major drought that resulted in serious food shortages. Famine was narrowly avoided by the arrival of food donated by other countries.

RAINFALL

Ghana is affected by two large air masses—one flows northward from the south Atlantic Ocean, while the other flows south from the Sahara Desert. The first is a humid, warm body of air that keeps day and night temperatures at around 77°F (25°C). The second is very dry and brings hot daytime temperatures, low nighttime temperatures, and clear skies.

Those two air masses effectively create regional weather conditions in Ghana. The extreme southwest of the country is the most influenced by the southern air mass. It receives about 75 inches (190 cm) of rain a year. As the air mass moves north, it loses water, so the northern part of the country receives much less rain. The Accra coastal plain has the lowest rainfall—from 40 inches (102 cm) a year to less than 30 inches (76 cm). There the land is flat, so the unobstructed clouds drift by without releasing any water.

Children playing in the almost round Lake Bosumtwi, situated within the bowl of a probable volcano.

WATER SYSTEMS

Ghana's river systems are fed by both rainfall and mountain springs. In the north of the country rivers that receive only rainwater are either flooded during the rainy season or are completely parched in the dry season. On the other hand, water volume in spring-fed streams shrinks in the dry season, but the streams do not dry up completely. In the forested zone, where rainfall is more consistent, the rivers flow throughout the year. In western Ghana several small rivers cut across the coastal plain as they drain into the Gulf of Guinea. The Pra, the Ankobra, and the Tano are the largest of those permanent rivers but are barely navigable as they have many rapids and waterfalls.

Ghana has only one natural lake, Bosumtwi in the south central interior. About 19 square miles (49 square km) in area, the lake is almost perfectly round and may have been formed by volcanic activity. It is surrounded by high hills. Streams in the hills feed Bosumtwi, many of them flowing around the lake before spilling into it.

There are also several lagoons. The largest of them is the one at Kéta in the southeast.

THE VOLTA RIVER Ghana's longest river is fed by three major tributaries. The Black Volta rises in Burkina Faso, where it is called the Baoule, travels along Ghana's border with Côte d'Ivoire, and empties into the Volta. The White Volta also rises in Burkina Faso, but flows almost due south to join the Volta. Both of those rivers are not navigable during the dry season, but flood during the wet season. Two major tributaries, the Afram and the Oti, also feed the Volta River. The Oti rises in Burkina Faso, crosses Togo, and enters Ghana to join the Volta.

In the 1960s the Volta was dammed from Akosombo in southeastern Ghana across to the town of Yapei is to create a hydroelectric power station. In operation by early 1966, it is 2,165 feet (660 m) long. A smaller dam at Kpong was built farther south, while the Black Volta also has been dammed, at Bui in the northwest of the country.

Lake Volta is among the world's largest artificial lakes. Covering 3,275 square miles (8,482 square km), its dam stands 407 feet (124 m) high. In addition to generating electricity and providing inland waterway transportation, Lake Volta is potentially valuable for irrigation and fish-farming.

Canoes ferry people to and from many landings along the Volta River.

FLORA AND FAUNA

Ghana is a lowland country but has three types of vegetation, which is largely determined by rainfall and human activity. In the southwest is the tropical rain forest where rainfall exceeds 65 inches (165 cm) annually. Farther east and north is a large band of deciduous forest.

Most of southern Ghana consists of evergreen and secondary forest—forestland that was once logged and cultivated but has since been reclaimed by the forest. Valuable African hardwoods such as mahogany, iroko (odum), and ebony are found there. Midway between deciduous forest and savanna, the region is the largest vegetation zone in Ghana, covering about 65,600

The rain forest in Ghana has three layers. Tall trees of 115-150 feet (35-46 m) form the canopy. These trees have wide crowns and buttresses at their roots to stabilize them in the shallow soil. A second group of trees with narrower crowns grow to heights of 50-80 feet (15-24 m). Below this is the underbrush consisting of young trees and plants that have adapted to survive in the deep shade of the forest floor. The underbrush is sparse so walking through the rain forest is relatively easy. Lianas and other climbing plants twine up the trees to reach sunlight.

THE BAOBAB TREE

The baobab is an unusual tree that the people of Ghana use in many ways. It grows throughout Africa in savanna areas and looks as if it has been turned upside down, with the branches buried in the soil and the roots sticking up in the air. The trunk can grow to a diameter of 30 feet (9 m) and as tall as 59 feet (18 m). Its mass of foliage can spread out to 150 feet (46 m) in diameter.

The fruit of the tree is large and gourdlike and can be eaten. The trunk is often hewn and hollowed out to make barrels used to collect and store rainwater. The bark can be made into rope and cloth, while the tree itself provides shade in many villages and is often the site of the village school.

square miles (170,000 square km). Trees found there include baobab, acacia, and shea tree. In the wet season such vegetation becomes very green. Tall grasses, up to 12 feet (3.7 m) high, cover the ground, waving gently in the breeze. In the dry season the trees lose their leaves and the grasses turn yellow.

The forest gradually gives way to the grasses and bushes of the savanna in the northern two-thirds of the country. The Black and White Volta rivers join to form the Volta, which runs south to the sea through a narrow gap in the hills.

In the southeast of the country around Accra is a stretch of coastal grassland of tall grass and scrub—stunted trees and bushes. This area receives little rain but is very humid. The few trees there include the drought- and fire-resistant baobab and nim, while in the wetter areas wild oil palms and fan palms grow.

Around the coastal lagoons and the Volta River in the southeast are mangrove swamps where the vegetation has adapted to living in saltwater. Mangrove trees grow to about 50 feet (15 m) and have tall aerial roots that help the plants remain upright in the soft mud of tidal waters.

Ghana has a rich and diverse animal life, although like the forests, that variety is seriously threatened because of the steadily encroaching human population. Ghana has over 200 species of mammals, including elephants, leopards, wild buffalo, antelope, and many kinds of primates, hyenas, and wild pigs. Once plentiful throughout the savanna, the elephants and lions are now rare and largely confined to nature reserves. Crocodiles and hippos are common along the rivers, and many species of poisonous snakes pose a danger to people. Cobras, puff adders, and horned adders can kill with their venomous bite, while pythons can squeeze their victims to death. More than 725 species of birds live in Ghana, from huge eagles to tiny swallows. Among the numerous birds are parrots, hornbills, kingfishers, herons, cuckoos, sunbirds, egrets, vultures, and snakebirds.

The Bamboo Cathedral in the Ankasa rain forest reserve is a stately experience for tourists.

MAJOR CITIES

ACCRA The capital city of Ghana since 1877, Accra has a population of 3 million. Located on the Gulf of Guinea, it is an old city that was first settled in 1471 when Portuguese sailors arrived in the area. Colonized in turn by the Dutch, English, and Danes in the 17th century, it grew into a prosperous trading center, blending contemporary and traditional African customs and architecture.

The administrative and financial center of Ghana, Accra possesses luxury hotels, fine restaurants, and lively entertainment. The heritage of Ghana from prehistoric to modern times is reflected in its cathedrals and museums dating from colonial times. The University of Ghana at Legon, founded in 1948, showcases Japanese architecture set in beautiful tropical gardens.

A soccer stadium and racecourse provide settings for sports, while Black Star Square is the center of cultural activities. On weekends tourists and resident Ghanaians head for the beaches along its shores, or take trains to beaches at other towns.

An aerial view of a wealthy suburb in Accra, revealing its colorful rooftops.

Set on hills and surrounded by forest, **Kumasi**, known as a garden city, has a humid climate with high rainfall.

The main industries of Accra are food processing and the manufacturing of textiles and lumber. Most of Ghana's imports arrive at Tema, 27 miles (43 km) to the east of the city center, and are then transported to Accra to be distributed around the country.

Like many cities in Africa, Accra has a mix of rich and poor. The relatively well-off own houses, cars, and electrical appliances, while others live with few possessions, poor sanitation, and scant comforts in shantytowns around the dismal edges of the city.

KUMASI This is Ghana's second-largest city, with a population of about 1.17 million (2000). Kumasi is located in south central Ghana, about 200 miles (322 km) northwest of Accra. An ancient city, it was the 17th-century capital of the Ashanti kingdom. Kumasi is situated at the junction of main roads and is the principal transit point for goods from the interior on their way to Accra and the seaports. This busy hub has teacher-training colleges, the University of Science and Technology, and agricultural research institutions.

The area around Kumasi is dedicated to cacao farming, which brings in much of the city's wealth. The Ashanti people, who still keep their capital at Kumasi, weave the colorful kente cloth, which is a profitable cottage industry. The city has an armed forces museum in an old British fort and also a cultural center. The largest market in all Ghana is spread out there, selling everything from handcrafts to auto parts. Traditional Ashanti buildings in Kumasi were designated a UNESCO World Heritage site in 1980.

A market in Tamale. This town acts as a distribution and collection center for the produce of the northern region. Cotton, rice, butter, and peanuts are gathered there and shipped to Accra. Tamale has a small airstrip, and there are plans for a larger airport. It also has a fruit-canning factory.

OTHER TOWNS The major town in the north of Ghana is Tamale, with a population of 350,000 (2009 estimate). It was developed as a town around 1907 when the British chose it as the administrative center of the northern region, a role it still holds. Other large towns in the north include Yendi and Bolgatanga, both built along main roads of the area. Bolgatanga is the most northerly major town of Ghana and has a population of about 49,000 (2000). It serves as an administrative center for the Frafra district.

Along the coast are a string of towns first established by European colonists, such as Sekondi-Takoradi, Cape Coast, Elmina, and Saltpond, with populations of 300,000 or less. A port city, Sekondi-Takoradi has an artificial harbor. It also has sawmills, paper factories, and an airport for light aircraft. Cape Coast is known as an educational center and has many schools and colleges as well as a university.

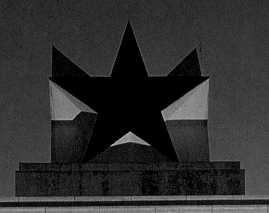

AD 1957

· FREEDOM AND JUSTICE ·

HISTORY

Black Star Square in Accra has been the site of many
public ceremonies since Ghana's independence in 1957

BEFORE INDEPENDENCE, THE country that is known today as Ghana was called the Gold Coast. The nation has had the name of Ghana only since independence in 1957. It took the name of an ancient kingdom far to the north of modern Ghana, and while many Ghanaians believe they are the descendants of that early empire, most historians believe otherwise.

Ghanaians enjoying the colorful ceremonies of Independence Day. Ghana was the first sub-Saharan African country to break the bonds of colonial rule.

EARLY HISTORY

Little is known about the early inhabitants of Ghana. Stone tools dating back to 5500—2500 B.C. found in the plains around Accra suggest a hunter-gatherer community of people who lived by the sea and moved around, gathering berries and wild seeds and hunting animals. The oral traditions of some tribes in Ghana also reveal a little about their early history. For example, stories by the Ewe people, who live in the southeast of Ghana, say that they emigrated to Ghana around A.D. 1600 after being driven out of modern Benin by another tribe. The Ga and Adangme, who live in the area around Accra, believe their ancestors came from southern Nigeria during the 16th century and conquered another tribe of people called the Guan. The Ga founded a small state called the kingdom of Accra, whose capital was inland from the modern city.

King John II (1455-95) of Portugal encouraged exploration of new lands and fostered trade with Africa.

The oral tradition of the inland Akan people tells that they first lived in Ghana around the 13th century in the northwest grasslands. As the Akan kingdom grew, groups migrated south to the forested areas and farther south to the coast.

ANCIENT TRADE ROUTES

Long before the arrival of Europeans to the west coast of Africa, those kingdoms traded with one another and with tribes from farther afield. The northwest trade route ran south from the ancient kingdom of Mali through modern Ghana and then south to modern Nigeria. From the busy trading town of Kumasi in central Ghana, more trade routes led to the coast. Along the trade routes came caravans carrying dates, salt, tobacco, and copper. The settlements of Ghana traded cloth, ostrich feathers, and tanned hides as well as cola nuts and slaves.

After 1591, great changes took place in Ghana's trading patterns, setting the future course of its history. That year war broke out between the Songhai Empire, Ghana's chief trading partner to the north, and the Moors of North Africa. As a result, the Songhai Empire fell into decline, bringing to a close the Ghanaians trade with the north.

ARRIVAL OF THE EUROPEANS

More than a century earlier, in 1471, Portuguese traders had arrived near Elmina on the southwest coast. Their original intention was to find a sea route to the lucrative markets of the Far East, and they sailed along the coast of Africa searching for such a passage. Venturing ashore, they discovered that the local people wore gold jewelry. The traders reported that news back to their King John II. In 1481 a special mission led by Diogo d'Azambuja was sent to Ghana. They found much gold and in 1482 built a fort at Elmina. Trade between Portugal and the tribes of Ghana flourished, with gold dominating the business. The Portuguese later built more forts—at Axim, Shama, and Accra—to store the gold while their trading ships were at sea and to protect the Portuguese traders and sailors from both the indigenous people and the English and Dutch, who were also exploring the area.

Elmina Castle, a legacy of the early Portuguese traders, is a **UNESCO** World Heritage Site.

In 1598 the Dutch began building forts at Mouri, Butri, Kormantsi, and Komeda, all along the southern coast of Ghana. Fierce competition between the Dutch and Portuguese for control of the area persisted, and in 1637 and 1642 the Dutch captured two Portuguese forts. During the 17th century the English, Germans, and Danes also built forts along the shore. Greedy for ivory and gold, they sailed in with shiploads of rum, cotton, beads, mirrors, and guns and gunpowder to exchange with the local people.

The European traders competed with one another for favor with the indigenous clans. They paid rent for their forts to the local chiefs and respected the chiefs' edicts that they not venture into the interior but remain in the coastal forts where trade goods were taken to them. Occasionally the Europeans were expected to lend a hand in intertribal battles.

THE ASHANTI

When the Akan people first migrated into Ghana, some settled around the confluence of the Pra and Ofin rivers. As their kingdom grew, some families moved north and founded the powerful Ashanti Empire in the Kumasi area.

A typical Ashanti village more than a hundred years ago.

During the 17th century a tribal chief named Osei Tutu formed an alliance of the various ethnic groups in the area. He built the capital town of Kumasi and designated a golden stool as his throne, a symbol of his power. He created a national army and expanded his empire, which he ruled well. Osei Tutu also astutely provided important jobs in his kingdom to the tribal leaders whom he had conquered. Other chiefs under his rule agreed to pay taxes for the purchase of guns and to travel to the capital whenever they were summoned.

In 1698 the Ashanti began a war with a neighboring kingdom, Denkyera. That kingdom stood between the Ashanti and the coast and controlled all trade of the Ashanti. After three years the Denkyera were defeated. In the reign of the next Ashanti king, Opuku Ware, more tribes in the interior were conquered until, by 1750, most of the tribes of the interior formed parts of the Ashanti Empire. The last kingdom to hold out against the onrush of the Ashanti was the Fanti Empire, which dominated the coastal area, and with it the prized trade with Europeans. In 1750, however, Opuku Ware died and civil war broke out among his potential successors. Several subject kingdoms seized the opportunity to declare their independence and joined the Fanti Empire. After that the Ashanti Empire began to decline, weakened by wars and a string of bad kings.

Osei Bosu became leader of the Ashanti in 1801, and under his rule the strength of the Ashanti grew once more. His armies finally defeated the Fanti in 1807, and the Ashanti became the most powerful empire in West Africa, controlling most of modern Ghana.

Portrait of an Ashanti horseman dressed in warrior finery.

When Europeans first began to trade with the people of Ghana, their chief interests were gold and ivory, but another commodity quickly became even more profitable. In the West Indies and in the colonies of the Americas, huge sugar and cotton plantations needed a source of cheap labor. The European slavers supplied the various ethnic groups with the guns and firepower that made possible the wars between the Ashanti and their tribal neighbors. Countless new slaves were taken in battle.

By the early 1700s slavery was the most important trade between the Europeans and the Africans. Ashanti raiding parties penetrated the interior and captured innocent people whom they herded to the coastal forts to sell. The forts became prisons, holding pens, and slave markets. Countless hundreds of people were thrown into the filthy holds of trading ships for the journey to the Americas. Many died from disease or starvation, or were murdered by the ships' captains.

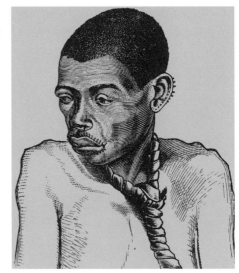

The vigorous slave trade continued for another hundred years, making the Ashanti the richest and most powerful empire in West Africa. The trade was finally stopped early in the 19th century, when first Denmark, then Britain, and finally America, in 1808, outlawed the slave trade and sent ships to capture the slave ships and return them with their human cargoes to Africa.

THE BRITISH IN GHANA

By the time the Europeans settled on the coast of Ghana, the British had developed trading relations with the Fanti tribe. They saw the growing power of the Ashanti as a threat to their own power. The Ashanti began attacking British forts, while the British provided military support to the Fanti. When the slave trade was finally abolished in Europe in the early 19th century, the British hoped that by destroying the Ashanti they could end the slave trade in Africa.

In 1821 a British governor was installed to administer the area, but he was killed by the Ashanti in 1824. The British eventually defeated the Ashanti in 1826. In 1829 George Maclean, a British military officer, was sent to Ghana to sign a peace treaty with the Ashanti. The British agreed to protect Ashanti traders and to arbitrate in intertribal disputes. On their part, the Ashanti and other tribes consented to stop human sacrifices and to keep the peace. In that new peace, trade again began to flourish. Palm oil, pepper, and corn were added to gold and ivory as valuable exports, while imports included tools, alcohol, tobacco, and guns.

In 1844 the British sent out a new governor to work with Maclean. The governor and his successors started raising taxes among the local ethnic groups to finance road building. That was very unpopular and led to attacks on British trading posts. In 1867 the British and Dutch agreed to divide the Ghanaian coast between them, with the British taking the east and the Dutch the west.

The British in a conference with Ashanti tribal chiefs in the 1870s.

A British officer receiving news of the Ashanti wars.

In 1868 the Fanti organized a confederation to oppose the British and to defend themselves against the Ashanti. The British saw this new alliance as a threat to their authority and arrested its leaders, leaving the confederation to fade away. The British began buying all the Dutch forts and by 1874 had become the sole European power in Ghana.

With the Fanti confederation weakened, the main remaining threat was the Ashanti, who lost their allies and source of guns when the Dutch left. The British attacked the Ashanti in 1874, burning their capital, Kumasi. Afterward, they initially allowed the Ashanti their independence, but in 1891, fearing that the French might annex the Ashanti territories, they declared the Ashanti kingdom a protectorate. The Ashanti challenged the declaration. In 1896 the British attacked Kumasi for the second time, exiling the ruler to Sierra Leone. During the 1890s the British extended their power to the north of Ghana, and by 1902, newly drawn borders formed the British colony named the Gold Coast.

THE 20TH CENTURY: A BRITISH COLONY

Ghana had only reluctantly become a colony in the British Empire. In the past the British had exerted only enough control to keep the exports flowing, but once Ghana was a colony, the priorities changed. A governor was appointed, with two councils (the legislative and executive councils), to help him make decisions. All the people who sat on these councils were British until 1914, when nine of the legislative councillors were Ghanaians. In 1943 two Africans joined the executive council. The legislative council functioned as a ratifying body for the laws that the governor introduced. By using a system of indirect rule, where the local chiefs acted as executives of the governor's laws, the British bypassed the intellectual elite of Ghana who might have challenged British authority if they were given any power.

In some ways the British brought peace and advancement to Ghana. The first gold mines were developed, where previously gold dust had been panned from rivers. Manganese, bauxite, and diamond mines were also created. Railways were built to carry the products of the mines to the coast, and harbors were constructed for the ships that came to collect the exports. The government distributed cocoa beans to local farmers and encouraged the cocoa industry. Towns sprang up as a result of trade and the railways, and in the growing towns the government also built hospitals and schools.

For many Ghanaians, however, those gestures were inadequate compensation for the massive profits that British companies were making from the labor of the Ghanaians. Until 1948 there were no universities in Ghana; if an African wanted a university education he had to go overseas to study.

GROWING NATIONALISM

One of the aspiring students who went abroad was Kwame Nkrumah. In the United States he studied Karl Marx and the writings of African Americans and developed radical ideas about independence for Ghana. In Ghana at that time there was already a pro-independence party that campaigned for a gradual shift to independence.

In 1947 Nkrumah broke away from that party and with the slogan "self-government now" shaped a more vocal and radical party, the Convention People's Party (CPP). In 1951, when Nkrumah was in jail for his party's campaign disturbances, the CPP won the general election. Nkrumah was released and asked to form a government. For six years Nkrumah and his party compromised, working with the colonial powers and at the same time learning about the workings of government. In 1957 power passed peacefully to the people of Ghana when Great Britain granted the country independence.

INDEPENDENCE AND BEYOND

Ghana was the first African colony south of the Sahara to gain political power; unfortunately, it went into a tailspin. At independence Ghana held half a billion U.S. dollars in reserves. Ten years later it was a billion dollars in debt. Foreign loans were taken out to finance ill-conceived projects such as the Akosombo Dam. Income plunged when the international price of cocoa collapsed. Many industries were nationalized and began losing money. From a peak of popularity throughout Africa in 1957, Kwame Nkrumah gradually resorted to one-party rule and ordered numerous arrests of political opponents to cling to power. An attempted coup failed in 1962, but in 1966, while he was abroad, another coup was successfully carried out. Nkrumah never returned to Ghana.

Between 1966 and 1981 a series of corrupt governments ran Ghana. For three years the government was run by a National Liberation Council and right-wing elements that hunted down left-wing politicians and parties. Nationalized industries were reprivatized. In 1969 elections were held and

The Kwame Nkrumah Memorial Tomb in Accra.

a politically moderate party took power. But the economy was so weak that food shortages and crushing price increases developed. In 1972 another takeover threw out that government. Military juntas seized power, food prices stayed high, corruption again became widespread, and political opponents were arrested.

In June 1979 yet another overthrow, led by Flight Lieutenant Jerry Rawlings, succeeded. That takeover was, however, different from the earlier coups. Rawlings had made the eradication of corruption his main promise—and kept his word. Many corrupt officials were arrested and executed and within a few months Rawlings had given up power and established a new democratically elected government. But that government fared little better than previous ones. A new set of corrupt politicians began siphoning off much needed state income.

In 1981 Rawlings led his second coup, promising once more to remove corrupt practices and restore stability to the economy. This time, Rawlings decided to keep the power and sort out the problems himself. Rawlings's ideas were very left wing. There were several attempts by other factions of the army to depose him, but all failed. Jerry Rawlings remained popular with Ghanaians at the grassroots level and himself oversaw a gradual improvement in the economy. In 1996 he held general elections and was reelected to office, a people's president in a stable country.

John Agyekum Kufuor was the next president, from 2001 until January 2009, when John Evans Atta Mills assumed that office.

Independence Square memorials in Accra.

GOVERNMENT

A citizen casts her vote during an election in Ghana.

INCE JANUARY 7, 2009, Ghana's government has been led by John Evans Atta Mills as the third president of the Fourth Republic. The former law professor from the National Democratic Congress (NDC) urged Ghanaians to unite for the socioeconomic development of their country. President Mills is the first Ghanaian democratic leader to lose power, stay in opposition for eight years, and then to win power back from an incumbent.

Supporters of Ghana's New Patriotic Party (NPP) gather before a campaign rally.

The State House of Ghana.

THE CONSTITUTION

Four constitutions have been adopted since Ghana's independence—the last in 1992, the current one. It calls for a multiparty system, with one legislative house of 200 members elected by direct, universal adult suffrage. The executive functions of the government are carried out by the president, a council of ministers approved by the legislature, and a vice president. There is also a National Security Council, made up of senior ministers and members of the security forces.

Beside the national government, there is a system of tribal governments led by chiefs.

THE PRESIDENT

The president is the head of state of Ghana and head of government. Jerry Rawlings, in 1992, was the first president to be elected under the current constitution. The president and vice president are elected on the same ticket by popular vote for a term of four years, with a possibility of a second term. In the December 7, 2008, election, there were eight candidates. None of them received a majority vote, so the electoral commission called for a runoff election. The outcome of the runoff was that president-elect John Evans Atta Mills (NDC) took 50.23 percent of the votes while Nana Akufo-Addo of the New Patriotic Party (NPP) claimed the remaining 49.77 percent.

Jerry John Rawlings was born in 1947 to a Scottish father and Ghanaian mother. He was educated in Ghana, first at Achimoto College and then at the military college. In 1969 he was commissioned a lieutenant in the air force. Ten years later he led a military coup against the corrupt civilian government of General Ignatius Kutu. Kutu and many others were tried and executed. Rawlings kept power for 112 days and then called a general election. Two years later, after the failure of the next president to prevent corruption or improve the economy, Rawlings led a second coup and this time held onto power, ruling with the aid of a Provisional National Defense Council.

Local committees were set up to monitor the work of factories and run local neighborhoods. In 1983 Rawlings switched from his Marxist policies to free-market ones, denationalizing state-owned industries, devaluing the currency, and abandoning price controls. All these measures were very unpopular, but people realized that he had Ghana's interests at heart and accepted them. Ghana become one of the few African countries with a healthy economy and relatively stable government under his presidency.

THE MINISTRIES

The council of ministers is made up of the heads of the various departments of state: the ministries of defense, state, finance, parliamentary affairs, foreign affairs, justice, local government, education, the interior, food and agriculture, health, roads and transportation, tourism, trade and industry, youth and sports, land and forestry, works and housing, communications, employment and social welfare, environment, science and technology, and mines and energy. The council ministers are nominated by the president, subject to approval by the parliament.

POLITICAL PARTIES

During the first decade of Rawlings's administration, political parties were banned in Ghana. They were legalized for the 1992 election, although none of Ghana's previous parties were allowed to register for the election. The New Patriotic Party (NPP) won the 2004 elections and governed for eight years under President John Kufuor. It lost by a narrow margin in the 2008 election that brought the National Democratic Congress (NDC) and President John Mills into power. A few smaller parties such as the Convention People's Party (CPP) and some independents form the opposition.

LOCAL GOVERNMENT

Democratically elected local governments were in place in Ghana in 1989. At the time, political parties were still banned and one-third of each district committee was appointed by the Rawlings government. Ghana is divided into ten regions, each with its own regional council.

The supreme court building in Accra.

THE JUDICIARY

The judicial system is based on English legal practice. In addition to statutory laws, there are customary laws and the English structure of common law, which is a series of laws not written down but accepted by the legal system. The superior courts are the supreme court, the court of appeal, the high court, and regional tribunals; the lesser courts are the circuit courts, district courts, and juvenile courts. Dissolved for a time during military rule, the supreme court has been reestablished as the court of final appeal. Its chief justice and ten other justices exercise jurisdiction over the interpretation and enforcement of the constitutional law. Outside of this system the Commission on Human Rights and Administrative Justice investigates corruption and abuse of public office.

TRIBAL GOVERNMENT

The traditional system of government in Ghana has outlasted numerous military and civilian governments as well as British rule. In ancient times each ethnic group had its own ruler who dominated life in his tribal area, often as small as a few villages but sometimes extending across the country. The chief ruled with the help of a council of elders and could call on the loyalty of the villages that he administered in time of war. Below that ruler were a

A local chief. The power of the tribal chiefs is restricted to tribal matters and traditional social customs.

Ghanaian soldiers marching during a parade. Men and women serve together in the armed forces.

series of local and village chiefs who sat on his council of elders and could depose a bad chief at will. The British used the tribal chieftaincies to wield control during colonial times, and the system remains in place today. Before the British came, the clan chief had power over all aspects of life and law. The British accepted the chiefs' rule over tribal matters but sat as a court of appeal when clan disputes threatened to escalate to war. Since independence in 1957, the successive national governments have retained this classic system in Ghana, while bit by bit reducing its power.

After 1957 Regional Houses of Chiefs were set up that elected representatives to sit in a national House of Chiefs. A ministry was set up to oversee tribal matters such as land rights and the appointment, removal, and succession of new chiefs. Even a separate judicial system has been used to adjudicate in disputes between individuals and their chiefs.

Ghana's recent foreign policy has emphasized good relations with its close neighbors. There is careful coordination of currencies, trade, infrastructure, and education with them within the Economic Community of West African States (ECOWAS). The rest of Africa and other countries also enjoy friendly relations with Ghana. Ghana practices economic diplomacy that facilitates trade, tourism, and investments in such key sectors as energy, agriculture and agro-processing, information and communication technology (ICT), infrastructural development (ports and roadways), and the tourist industry. President John Evans Atta Mills and U.S. President Barack Obama conferred during Obama's July 2009 visit to Ghana.

THE ARMY

Since 1957 the army has played a leading role in the government of Ghana. For 25 years, the army was responsible for many coups: all have been relatively popular and targeted at corrupt civil governments. The armed forces of 7,000 troops, composed of both men and women, is comparatively small. Only 0.8 percent of the GDP (gross domestic product) is spent on the military, compared with a world average of 2.5 percent, or $202 for each person in the world.

GHANA'S FIRST LEADER

Kwame Nkrumah, Ghana's first prime minister and, later, president, was a powerful and popular leader. He was born in 1909 in what was then the British Gold Coast colony. After teaching in the colony for some years, Nkrumah left for Lincoln University in the United States to study politics, particularly the theories of Marx, Lenin, and Marcus Garvey, the 1920s black Jamaican leader who worked for years in the United States in the cause of all blacks. Nkrumah returned to the Gold Coast in 1947 at the invitation of the United Gold Coast Convention (UGCC), a party agitating for independence.

He became very popular, speaking at meetings all over the country. In 1948, after several riots, Nkrumah was arrested, along with other UGCC leaders, on suspicion of organizing the riots but was soon released. Later he split with the UGCC, which he considered too middle class, and founded a new party based on a principle of immediate self-government, the Convention People's Party (CPP). In 1950 he orchestrated a series of demonstrations, strikes, and noncooperation activities. In the ensuing civil disruption, Nkrumah was arrested for the second time and sentenced to a year's imprisonment.

Kwame Nkrumah wearing traditional Ghanaian dress, including the beloved kente cloth fabric.

In 1951, while still in jail, Nkrumah was elected to parliament in a massive demonstration of political support, and in 1952 the people's champion became prime minister of the Gold Coast. He served as prime minister for five years under British rule and oversaw the peaceful transformation to independence. His style of government then changed abruptly, and he began imprisoning people without trial. Nevertheless, his public building programs kept him popular with ordinary countrymen. In 1960 he became president of the Republic of Ghana under Ghana's second constitution.

Always interested in black African politics, President Nkrumah began to champion the idea of African unity—a single African state of massive size and power. His development projects grew more and more expensive and unrealistic, and soon Ghana was in debt to foreign powers. As dissent grew,

Born on July 21, 1944, President John Evans Atta Mills came from Ekumfi Otuam in Central Region. He earned his bachelor's degree and Professional Certificate of Law (1967) from the University of Ghana, Legon. While working on his doctorate in Oriental and African Studies at the University of London, the 27-year-old student was selected as a Fulbright Scholar at Stanford University Law School in California. Upon graduation, Professor Mills made his mark at the Faculty of Law at University of Ghana, Legon. A prolific writer, he also presented research papers at symposiums and conferences throughout the world. John Evans Atta Mills has more than a dozen publications on taxation and other law fields to his credit and has held senior positions with finance-related institutions throughout Ghana. He remains enthusiastic in recreation and sports.

President Mills's previous achievements included being Acting Commissioner of the Internal Revenue Service of Ghana (1988). From 1997 to 2000 he served as vice president of the Republic of Ghana, with President Jerry Rawlings.

Although Mills also ran in the 2000 and 2004 presidential elections, he lost both times to the NPP candidate, John Agyekum Kufuor, the outgoing president. On January 3, 2009, John Atta Mills was sworn into office as executive president of the Republic of Ghana. He is married to Ernestina Naadu, an education specialist. They have a 19-year-old son.

Nkrumah began to exert his political control in an increasingly draconian way. An attempt was made on his life in 1962, and he withdrew from public view. Ghana became a one-party state, and food shortages made life hard for Ghanaians everywhere. While on a visit to Beijing in 1966, Nkrumah was deposed by the police and army. He died in exile in 1972 in Romania while receiving treatment for throat cancer.

ECONOMY

Mammy wagons, or *tro tros* (TRO-tros), play an important role in the day-to-day lives of farmers, helping them to transport products to the city markets.

CHAPTER 4

N RECENT YEARS GHANA has enjoyed one of the healthiest economies in Africa and is an example of successful economic recovery and political reform on the continent. Shortly after independence Ghana's economy suffered greatly at the hands of rulers with grandiose programs and corrupt administrations.

From the strongest economy in 1957 it became one of the poorest countries in Africa. Kwame Nkrumah's policies of nationalization—having many state-owned enterprises—and huge cash outlays on projects such as the Akosombo Dam resulted in a serious decline in production and a drop in per capita income. Poor planning and a shortage of capital and managerial skills were the main factors in that dire economic situation. The military governments and ineffective civilian rule that followed worsened the situation.

A crane loading a container onto a truck at the port of Sekondi-Takoradi.

The stability of the Jerry Rawlings years and tough economic policies have helped reverse Ghana's decline and have sparked renewed foreign interest in investing in the country's renewal. Subsequent governments have had to arrest inflation, reschedule overseas debt repayment, increase agricultural productivity, and encourage exportation of locally manufactured goods. Conditions were looking much better by the 1990s.

Ghana has always been rich in natural resources, especially gold. Industries based on those resources are back in production. The Rawlings administration sought the help of the International Monetary Fund, which recommended an economic recovery program aimed at a free-market economy, tight control of spending, and the removal of subsidies for staple foods. Although unpopular, those straightforward measures have won acceptance.

Ghana's economy, a mixture of private and public enterprise, is based on agriculture and mining, and its chief exports are gold and cocoa. Accra has become the main artery through which Ghana's exports are moved and luxury commodities enter the country.

Many African countries are producers of primary products, such as minerals and crops, and their well-being depends on world commodity prices that are controlled by markets far away in the international financial centers. Prices can fall and wipe out a country's income. For instance, in the mid-1960s cocoa prices collapsed, pushing Ghana's economy into serious decline.

Cranes filling trucks with gold ore rubble after blasting, on its way to processing.

AGRICULTURE

Sixty percent of Ghana's workforce is employed in agriculture, and over a third of the nation's economy is in agriculture.

Besides cocoa, Ghana also produces rice, cassava (tapioca), peanuts, corn, shea nuts, bananas, and timber. Bananas were first exported from Ghana in 1929. They are grown in the southeast, in the forested region where the weather is warm and humid. Banana production is difficult because the fruit is delicate and easily damaged. It has to be picked when unripe and kept in special cool containers. Fortunately, in Ghana the growing areas are near the southern seaports, so the bananas can be transported quickly and are less likely to be damaged.

Cola nuts, the basic ingredient of the many cola drinks consumed around the world, is a lucrative industry in Ghana. The trees they grow on need the same environment as cocoa, so the two crops may compete for the same available space on farms. Cola trees, however, grow faster and so are used as shade trees for young cacao plants—the two plants are often seen growing together.

Coconuts are grown along the coast. They were first grown commercially after 1920 when the British colonial government set up plantations and nurseries and distributed seedlings to local farmers to encourage the crop. The main product of coconut trees is copra, the dried meat of its fruit, from

Workers washing bananas at a banana plantation in Ghana.

The shea tree grows wild in Ghana. It produces shea nuts, which yield shea butter, used in the manufacture of soap, candles, and some foods.

COCOA

Cocoa is Ghana's most important cash crop and its highest export earner, accounting for some two-thirds of the country's revenue. It provides employment to more than half a million people. Cocoa also provides much of the capital for Ghana's many infrastructure projects. Cocoa was first exported in 1885. In 1890 the colonial government set up a botanical garden to raise cacao seedlings to distribute to local farmers. It is cultivated mostly in forested regions because it needs deep, well-drained soil and a high rainfall throughout the year, although too much rain at any one time can induce disease in the plant.

The cacao crop is first cultivated on forestland that has been cleared of all but the few trees kept to shade the young plants. Additional shade comes from cocoyams and plantains, which also help provide some income while the cacao trees are still small. The trees become productive after about five years. At that stage the enterprise becomes labor-intensive. Harvesting, which can take three or four months, begins in September. The large, ripe cocoa pods are collected and the beans scooped out and fermented for several days. They are then sun-dried for about two weeks and packed into bags for shipment to processors.

which coconut oil is processed. Tobacco is one of the smallest cash crops in Ghana. It has been grown commercially since the 1930s, cultivated in small pockets in various parts of the country. A tobacco company was established in Ghana in 1951.

Sugarcane is grown mostly on a small-scale basis by individual farmers; there are few commercial sugarcane plantations in Ghana. The plant needs plenty of rainfall to thrive and therefore is grown in valleys or in the forested region. Cultivated mostly for domestic consumption, it is also used by the alcohol industry. Factories sited near plantations convert the juice to sugar.

Besides those commercial products, many other crops are grown and either consumed within the villages or sold at local markets. They include corn, millet, groundnuts (peanuts), tomatoes, green vegetables, peppers, cocoyam (a root vegetable), cassava, yams, and plantains.

FISHING AND LIVESTOCK

Fishing is a small domestic industry. Families living along the coast go out in canoes to catch fish to supplement their diet. Larger commercial boats are motorized and use nets to catch tuna, bream, and herring. A state fishing agency operates a fleet of trawlers, and there are some private foreign-owned fishing fleets. In the north of the country there are a few small fish farms. Lake Volta provides a useful supply of freshwater fish. The many lagoons along the coast are another source of seafood. Tema, 16 miles (26 km) from Accra, is Ghana's largest fishing port.

Fishermen at harbor with their colorful boats and nets.

Poultry farms are now common in Ghana, as chicken has become a staple dish and is the celebration meal of choice.

Cattle are raised commercially on a small scale in the coastal savanna areas such as the Accra Plains. The total head of cattle produced, however, falls far short of demand, and most of the beef consumed in Ghana is imported. The drier northern region is ideal for raising cattle, but there cattle traditionally represent wealth. Therefore, many thousands of cattle are herded but usually not for meat, being too valuable to eat. Raising cattle is difficult in many areas because of seasonal water shortages and because no feed crop is grown.

MANUFACTURING

Countries that have developed manufacturing industries have far more stable economies than countries that depend on primary production such as agriculture. World prices of manufactured goods are more unchanging than those of staples. Establishing a manufacturing base, though, is expensive and risky, with high outlays in infrastructure, research and development, workforce training, and the much more complex administration needed for manufactured goods. When Ghana was a colony, all primary products were exported to Britain and processed there. After independence both local entrepreneurs and the various governments realized the importance of developing a manufacturing base. Nonetheless, by 1960 only 8.6 percent of the working population was engaged in manufacturing.

The Rawlings government created a climate conducive to investment; as a result manufacturing has grown by about 9 percent a year. By the 1990s manufacturing amounted to 14 percent of the GNP (gross national product). The sector declined steadily from a GDP of 9.02 percent in 2000 to 8.1 percent in 2007, reflecting the worldwide energy crisis. In 2008 manufacturing output was at 25.3 percent (GDP) as a result of foreign capital and joint ventures. Ghana's food-processing industries include sugar refineries, flour mills, and several cocoa-processing factories where Ghanaian chocolate is made. The country also has beef-processing plants, dairy products works, vegetable-oil mills that produce coconut and palm oil, and small tomato and pineapple factories. There are several breweries making beer from imported hops, a soft-drink industry, and cigarette factories.

Cotton is grown in Ghana as well as imported. Cotton fibers are woven into cloth and then into clothing in factories ringed around the southern cities. Jute, kenaf, and roselle are other fiber plants grown in Ghana that are turned into cloth, rope, and sacks in small factories.

The forestry industry supports sawmills, furniture and boat building, and the manufacture of plywood and paper products. Ghana also has oil refineries that process kerosene, gasoline, and diesel fuel; cement works and brick factories using imported materials; and chemical plants that make medicines, insecticides, and paints.

Women working in an apparel factory in Ghana. Most such apparel is sold locally, but some Afrocentric clothing is exported.

Lumber being treated and cut in a sawmill in Kumasi.

ELECTRICITY

Before 1966 when the Akosombo hydroelectric plant at the foot of Lake Volta was opened, electricity was produced by small diesel generators. The new power plant supplied electricity to Accra and the towns of southern Ghana. Most of its newfound electric power went to the aluminum smelting plant nearby, but for several years the power supply was inadequate because of operating problems and a series of droughts.

Since 1981 the system has been improved and extended. Now almost all the major towns receive electricity, and Ghana even sells electricity to neighboring countries.

MINING AND FORESTRY

Gold, diamonds, manganese, and bauxite are mined in Ghana. Gold mining slumped after independence, but the beautiful metal has recently begun to catch up with cocoa as a leading export. Ghana's diamonds are mostly of industrial grade rather than as jewelry. The nation is also the world's eighth-largest producer of manganese, with mines in the western region. There are large reserves of bauxite in Ghana, but the mining of it is not developed, and most of the raw bauxite used in aluminum manufacturing is imported. In recent years foreign companies have shown an increasing interest in Ghana's

Railways extend across the country, linking major production areas with Accra. The railways are largely used to move freight. Schedules are irregular so trains are unpopular as public transportation. Many of Ghana's rivers are not navigable, but the dam at Akosombo has created the huge Lake Volta that makes water transportation from the north cheap and convenient. Ports have been built around the lake to facilitate this increasingly popular mode of travel. Ghana has small airports at Takoradi, Kumasi, Sunyani, and Tamale, in addition to the Kotoka International Airport in Accra.

mineral resources. A small deposit of offshore oil has also been discovered, but as yet there is not enough to make commercial extraction worthwhile.

Ghana's forest reserves have been exploited for decades, particularly during the 1960s. After a decline in production in the 1970s and 1980s, the country's timber resources are now being managed well and exports are on the rise. Ghana has projected sufficient reserves until the year 2030.

TRANSPORTATION

Ghana's chief means of transportation are roads, railways, rivers, Lake Volta, and air. In the more rural and undeveloped north of the country horses and donkeys are still used. Transportation routes are linked in the major areas of economic production, connecting them with urban centers and ultimately with Accra. Roads for cars and trucks were first constructed in the early years of the 20th century, linking the southern towns, and then they were extended to the cacao plantations in the southwest.

Like much of Ghana's economy, the road system was not kept up during the 1970s and 1980s, but since then many roads have been paved and cared for. Asphalt roads string along the coast, joining the coastal towns, and lead to Kumasi in the center of Ghana and then northward to Tamale. Similar roads link the other major towns. A two-lane freeway runs from Accra to Tema, though it is only 16 miles (26 km) long. Other roads are smaller and unsurfaced and are often swept away altogether in the rainy season, making travel difficult.

ENVIRONMENT

Palm trees growing next to plots of rice paddies.

CHAPTER 5

THE ENERGY CRISIS AND recurrent drought in Ghana severely affect its economy and agricultural activities. Ghanaians saw the colossal hydropower project on the Volta River as the answer. In addition to generating electric power for industry and household energy needs, it was meant to provide large-scale irrigation and modernization of agriculture, and even promote tourism.

The magnificient red hues of the sunset on the Volta River.

Mike Anane, founder of the League of Environmental Journalists in Ghana, published the book *Covering the Environment–A Guide to Environmental Journalism in Developing Countries.* Through his articles and workshops he encourages the media to take a more serious interest in raising awareness of destructive problems such as toxic waste dispersal in Ghana and other countries around the world.

Construction of the dams may have solved some problems but at the same time created big new ones, such as flooding, waterborne diseases, and the lamentable sacrifice of wildlife habitats. Modernization comes with a price tag to the environment.

TOXIC WASTES

The U.S. Environmental Protection Agency (EPA) estimates that 30 to 40 million personal computers a year are ready for "end-of-life management" when memory and graphic demands escalate beyond the capacity of the computer. Other consumer electronics such as televisions and cell phones exacerbate the massive problem. That results in a new, deadly kind of waste—electronic waste. It is almost impossible to gauge how much electronic waste is dumped in West African countries such as Ghana, Nigeria, and Côte d'Ivoire from Europe and other countries.

Along the sidewalks of Agbogbloshie Market in Accra, battered Pentium 2 and 3 computers, broken monitors, old television sets that receive only analog signals, VCRs, cell phones, and other digital hardware and equipment are piled 10 feet (3 m) high. Working items are put up for sale; loads of old broken

Local children pumping clean, filtered water for their families.

ones are sold for a pittance to scrap dealers, who make their living stripping off resalable components such as drives, memory chips, copper, and other metals to make a dollar or two from a scrap-metal buyer. What cannot be exchanged for money is burned. Tires are used for fuel to burn the valueless relics, releasing carcinogens and other toxic particles into the air. While the adults collect and count their gains, children tend to the burning piles, sending great pillars of lethal black smoke billowing up. The scrap dealers, most of them either related or friends, scurry through the acrid haze feeling sick in the head and chest, compromising health and safety when speed is the key to making money. Discarded parts that cannot turn to ash are thrown into the lagoon to be flushed out to the Gulf of Guinea by the rain.

The shipping and dumping of toxic waste in the country exposes Ghanaian children to high levels of lead, phthalates, and chlorinated dioxins that are known to promote cancer and to cause other impediments to natural health. Environmental experts in Ghana are educating the public and urging the electronic industry to phase out toxic chemicals in the making of their products or to set up recycling programs to safely dispose of the remains.

Old computers from Europe and the United States are dumped in Ghana where the computer parts are burned to recover copper and other metals, creating toxic air pollution.

Construction of a dam on the Volta River began in the early 1960s, and the dam was in operation by 1966. The lake that was created behind it stretches 250 miles (400 km). The long, thin Lake Volta flooded 2.1 million acres (850,000 hectares) of inhabited land (one-seventh of Ghana's total landmass), and 80,000 people had to be resettled. The hydroelectric power generated by the Akosombo Dam supplies a power grid covering southern Ghana and extending into Togo.

The lake provides an inland waterway system that reduces the cost of transporting goods from the north to the south of the country. Its waters irrigate parts of the Accra Plains, which had no steady source of water, and it has added huge numbers of fish to the country's fishing stocks. It is likely too, in the long run, to affect the country's climate by making the area more humid and increasing rainfall.

EFFECTS OF DAM PROJECTS

Regular droughts over the past three decades have resulted in an erratic power supply, which also severely affected agricultural activities in Ghana. The giant Volta River Project, encompassing the Akosombo and Kpong dams built in the 1960s and 1970s, provided the much needed electricity to sustain Ghana's rapid domestic and industrial power needs in the early independent years. The impoundment of the Volta River at the two sites, however, has also caused a reduction in the flow of the river, both upstream and downstream. That slowdown has resulted in an invasion of aquatic weeds that today squeezes navigable space, causing silting and closure of the estuary where the Volta meets the Gulf of Guinea.

Most of Ghana's power supply comes from its dams. Another large dam is being built at Bui on the Black Volta River to minimize Ghana's dependence on imported fuel. The Bui Dam project—expected to be completed in 2012—would submerge a quarter of the 700 square miles (1,813 square km) of Bui National Park, home to more than a hundred rare black hippopotamuses and species

This flood in Ghana caused some 260,000 local people to lose their homes, crops and roads.

Freshly cut tree trunks are left to dry in one of the many sawmills found in Kumasi.

of monkeys, lions, buffalo, monitor lizards, antelope, and leopards. Naturalists believe that the animals will be forced to migrate to an area near agricultural lands where conflict with farmers could result. The altered flow of the Black Volta would also negatively impact the habitats of 46 species of fish that are economically important to local Ghanaians. Prolonged drought from climate change could severely constrain the dam's capacity. The government has promised to work alongside a variety of agencies to mitigate the negative environmental, social, and ecological impact of dam projects.

DEFORESTATION

Hardwood forests covered half of Ghana in the late 19th century. Today, farming activities and timber exploitation have reduced a dense forest zone of about 30,000 square miles (78,000 square km) to less than 8,000 square miles (21,000 square km). That is the result of clearing large tracts of forest for cacao plantations, which thrive in the deep, rich soil of the forest. During times of depressed cocoa prices, timber is sold abroad to generate needed revenue. Although Ghana bans the export of raw logs and about 5 percent of the land is officially protected, illegal logging threatens the country's remaining forests.

Deforestation also depletes wildlife populations by habitat loss. Since 1988, Ghana has put in place conservation plans and ratified international agreements protecting its forests and endangered species, biodiversity, and the ozone layer.

EROSION

Like many other countries where the population is growing, the land in Ghana is coming under increasing pressure as villages expand and the soil becomes depleted. Improved irrigation in the Voltaian Basin encouraged people to raise cattle, and because of this profitable work, large areas of the savanna are being denuded due to overgrazing.

Forested areas are being logged off and turned into grassland, which in turn becomes infertile and overgrazed. The result is erosion, as torrential rains fall on what once was vegetation but is now barren soil. Much of the rain forest that has been logged has not been replanted. The government has designated protected reserves where trees cannot be logged and where animals are safe from hunters. Similar solutions will have to be found for the grasslands and cultivated land around the major cities, where the soil is not left fallow (idle) long enough for vegetation to reestablish itself.

GHANAIANS

A Ghanaian woman surrounded by brilliant flowers.

ABOUT 23 MILLION PEOPLE (2008) live in Ghana, belonging to over 50 different ethnic groups, each with its own language and customs. For all those differences, Ghana is a nation of ethnic harmony, with very few instances of conflict brought about by cultural differences.

The Akan tribes form the largest ethnic group in Ghana, making up about 45 percent of the population. The Akan are not a single ethnic group, however, and they speak many dialects of their common language, Twi. The Twi peoples live mainly in the southern half of the country.

Ghana has a fairly young population, with 37 percent of the population under the age of 15.

Ghana is a remarkably egalitarian society with a tribal structure. Kinship loyalties are prevalent throughout the country.

The northern clans, Mole-Dagbon, are more diverse and make up about 15 percent of the population. They have different, unrelated, languages but also speak a common tongue, Dagbane. The Ewe groups live in the Volta region and make up about 12 percent of the population. The Ga-Dangme, who make up 7 percent of the population, live mostly in the coastal area around Accra. There is also a small number of other groups.

Another significant division among the peoples of Ghana is that of town and country. About 65 percent of the population lives in the countryside, while 35 percent lives in the cities. That division changes continually in favor of city life, as more and more people take manufacturing and commercial jobs instead of holding onto agricultural ones. About 45 percent of the population is counted as being economically active, meaning that they take part in the market economy rather than living by subsistence farming. About 56 percent of the working population is in agriculture, while 37.5 percent is in service industries such as business, trade, or tourism. The average family size is comparatively low for Africa, at 4.9 people per household.

Knife grinders ready for customers in a city market. Many men have moved to urban centers seeking a modern lifestyle.

Ghana does not have the social distinctions based on class or wealth that exist in many European countries. It is essentially an egalitarian society with a tribal structure. Within the tribes all men are equal, however rich they may be, although in some clans only certain families may become chiefs. But the chiefs are chosen by the people, who can "destool" or unseat an unpopular chief, removing him from command.

In many of the tribes property and land are owned by families, not individuals, and is continually redistributed among the family, so few people ever build up personal fortunes or estates. Conversely, few people are really destitute or without family to support them, because everyone has a larger group they can, count on in times of trouble.

THE AKAN

The Akan tribes, the largest ethnic group in Ghana, live in the southwest and central areas of the country. Subgroups within the Akan group include the Brong, Banda, Adanse, Assin, Twifo, Denkyera, Akyem, Wassa, Akwamu, and Ashanti. The Akan tribes originally lived in the savanna areas in the northwest of Ghana and the northeast of Côte d'Ivoire. They traded cola nuts and gold, which they panned from the rivers, with the people of the coast. They all speak various dialects of the Twi language. Their lives today are still organized around village communities, with the majority surviving on subsistence farming. Nevertheless, many have migrated to the towns and taken up a modern, urban lifestyle.

A modern Ashanti family in Ghana.

A Fanti chief in Cape Coast.

Many Fanti have migrated to the coast or reside in other West African countries.

A subgroup of the Akan are the Fanti (also spelled Fante), who live on the southern coast between Accra and Sekondi-Takoradi. Their oral tradition reports that they moved to the coast from the Ashanti region in the 17th century. They grow cassava, cocoyam, and plantains. Many also have small commercial ventures in cocoa, palm oil, and timber.

THE NORTHERN ETHNIC GROUPS

The Dagomba are one of the major ethnic groups in the north. They are believed to have migrated from east of Lake Chad, across modern Nigeria, and into their present homeland in the north central region of Ghana. The Dagomba speak a Niger-Congo language and are farmers, growing yam, sorghum, millet, corn, and groundnuts. They also raise cattle and other livestock and live in walled villages. They are among the least affected by modern life.

The Mamprusi occupy the East and West Mamprusi districts of northern Ghana in the area between the Nasia River and the White Volta. They used to be known in English as Dagomba, but since their southern neighbors appropriated the name, they changed theirs to Mamprusi. They speak several Mole-Dagbani languages. Their individual homes are in circular compounds in areas of vegetation known as orchard bush. They are farmers, cultivating crops such as millet, corn, hibiscus, rice, and tobacco. Like the Dagomba, their songs tell of a time when they lived near Lake Chad and migrated to Ghana.

Another ethnic group, the Guan, live in the area where the Black Volta and White Volta rivers merge. Strangely, in that clan the rulers speak a different language than the ordinary people. The Guan live in small villages of fewer than 300 people and practice shifting cultivation, that is, farming a piece of land until it is barren and then moving on.

The Fulani are a nomadic band who live throughout West Africa. They speak Fulfulde. Those in Ghana are chiefly herdsmen for hire, looking after the cattle of northern ethnic groups.

OTHER ETHNIC GROUPS

The Ewe live in southeastern Ghana as well as in Benin and the southern half of Togo. Their original home was in modern Benin, but they were driven out by the expansion of the Yoruba Empire in the 16th century. They speak a version of the Kwa language and are farmers and fishermen as well as potters and blacksmiths.

An Ewe woman in traditional dress. Unlike most of the other tribes of Ghana, the Ewe never formed a single central domain.

The Ga also live in southeastern Ghana. They are coastal people whose language belongs to part of the Ga-Adangebe language system. They arrived in Ghana in the 17th century, making their way down the Niger River and across the Volta River. They established the towns of Accra, Osu, Labadi, Teshi, Nunga, and Tema, each new town with a stool as its symbol of leadership and a chief to go with it. Originally farmers, the Ga have branched out into fishing and trade. Unusual among Ghanaians, the main breadwinner in a Ga family is the woman.

A woman in a traditional dress of kente cloth.

Speaking very similar dialects is a group of tribes called the Adangme. They live along the Volta and part of the coast. They are farmers, growing millet, cassava, yams, corn, plantain, and some cash crops.

DRESS

In cities of southern Ghana the typical dress is Western style, with shorts and T-shirts for most men or a suit and tie for businessmen. Women wear dresses or pants cut from imported, patterned cloth or local traditional designs. During elections, funerals, or important political or religious functions, Ghanaians often wear clothes with images of their political leaders to honor them. The traditional cloth of Ghana is called kente cloth. Narrow strips of cloth are woven on small looms and sewn together by hand to make several yards of material. Each pattern woven into the cloth has a story and significance for the various tribes. Women in the cities may have their kente cloth made into dresses, skirts, and blouses.

Traditional styles of dress vary from region to region. In the north live many Muslims, and their clothing reflects their religious beliefs. Men wear loose-flowing, full-length robes, usually blue, white, or a dark color.

In the south the cloth is patterned in bright colors. A man's traditional attire is made of 26 to 33 feet (8 to 10 m) of cloth draped in a very specific way and often worn over a shirt and shorts. At funerals the common color to wear is black. It is also appropriate to wear red at the funerals of relatives. White, which represents joy and victory, can be worn at the death of an octogenarian or older. The women must wear a black cloth wound around their head.

HOW TO WEAR A GHANAIAN MAN'S TRADITIONAL DRESS

1. *Take 33 feet (10 m) of cloth and drape it around the back, with the left arm in line with the top selvedge and the right arm above the top selvedge.*

2. *Gather the cloth in the left hand over the left shoulder.*

3. *Take the cloth in the right hand under the right arm and pull it forward over the left shoulder. Both ends of the cloth are now over the left shoulder.*

4. *Bring forward the bulk of the cloth, hanging behind the left shoulder, and throw over the left shoulder again. This leaves the right arm and shoulder bare.*

Women's traditional dress consists of three garments and a girdle, or sash. The first is a loose blouse. The second is a large piece of cloth wrapped around the waist, forming a floor-length skirt. The blouse is tucked into the girdle, which holds up the skirt. Above this the woman wraps the third of her garments, another piece of cloth, which is tied around the waist, and then folded over the left shoulder. This third piece can be used to carry a baby. Most women wear some form of headdress, either a scarf tied simply around the head or a more elaborately designed turban.

KINGSLEY OFOSU

In October 1992 nine young Ghanaian men from Takoradi decided to seek their fortunes in the West and stowed away on a boat named the *MC Ruby*. Four days before arriving in Le Havre, France, the stowaways were discovered by the Ukrainian crew, taken out on deck and shot, and the bodies of eight of them were thrown into the sea. One, Kingsley Ofosu, who had head injuries from the attack, eluded the crew and spent the four days being hunted around the ship. Once in Le Havre he escaped and reported the murders of his brother and his friends to the authorities.

After a long trial the Ukrainian crew members were sentenced to life imprisonment. The survivor, Kingsley Ofosu, was offered a chance to stay in France and study engineering. That might have been the end of a tragic affair, except that American actor Danny Glover heard the story and decided to make a movie about Ofosu's experiences. The rights to his story made Ofosu a wealthy man by Ghanaian standards, and he became both rich and famous because of his terrible ordeal. The Ghanaian premiere of the 1996 movie, called *Deadly Voyage*, raised the money to build a rehabilitation center in Takoradi to help the many repatriated stowaways who have had less horrific experiences than Ofosu, but who nevertheless failed to make their fortunes in the West.

Kingsley Ofusu after the trial of his attackers in France.

KOFI ANNAN

Kofi Annan, a Ghanaian, became internationally well-known in 1997 when he was made the United Nations secretary-general. His term of office began with a crisis in Iraq, where UN weapons inspectors were in dispute with the Iraqi government over access to certain areas. Secretary-General Annan was able to defuse what might have developed into a very dangerous situation, as American and British troops were poised to attack Iraq.

Annan was a career official in the United Nations. He joined the World Health Organization in 1962 as a clerk in Geneva and, after 30 years of service, was nominated to its highest position. He was educated in the United States and Switzerland. His job at the United Nations came at a time of crisis for the world organization. The UN's role was no longer well-defined in a post—Cold War era, and it was seriously in debt. About half the member states were not paying their contribution to its upkeep, including the United States, which owed over one billion dollars. Kofi Annan served nine years as secretary-general, resigning in 2006.

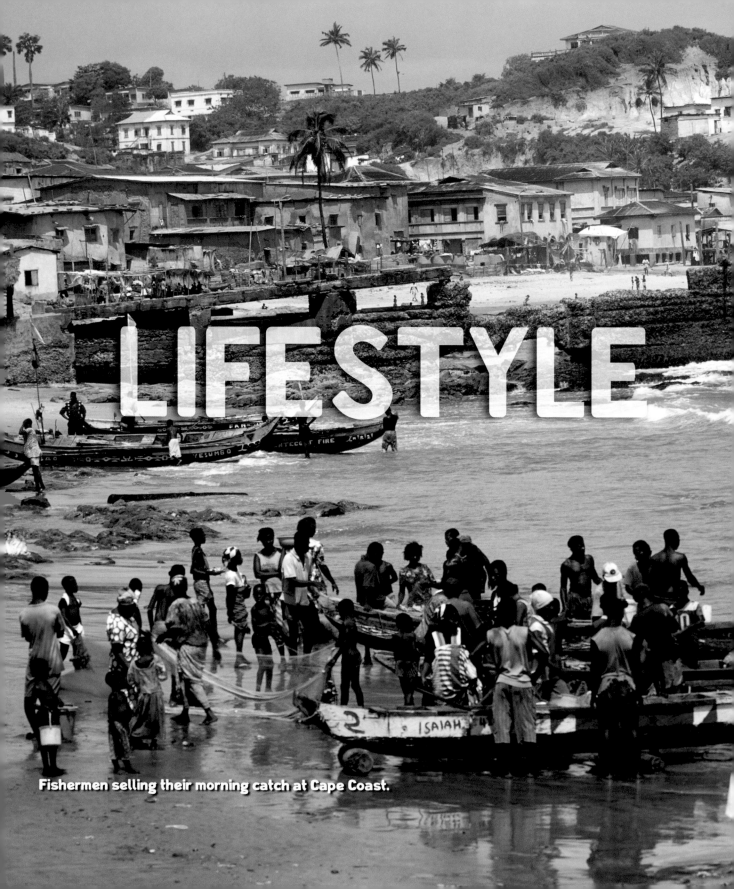

LIFESTYLE

Fishermen selling their morning catch at Cape Coast.

G HANA SAW TREMENDOUS CHANGE in social structures and lifestyles in the 20th and early 21st centuries. In many rural areas the threads that once bound society together have frayed as Ghanaians move away from a subsistence economy to a managed economy. In the cities wealth, migration, education, and new expectations have led to a society based on the nuclear family, supplanting the clan.

Computer literacy has been steadily improving in modern Ghana.

Enormous differences in wealth, education, health care, housing, expectations, and opportunities exist in the country.

The changes brought about in economic policy have doubtless improved the lives of many citizens, particularly those living in the south and people employed in manufacturing and trade. But life remains hardscrabble for others, especially in the far north, where drought has brought extreme poverty and malnutrition. Several charities serve in Ghana. One of them is ActionAid, which works mainly in the north of the country, providing loans, seed, education, and health care. Another is The Fight Against Guinea Worm Disease, which is led and funded by the Carter Center in Ghana, founded by Jimmy Carter, former president of the United States.

TRADITIONAL SOCIAL STRUCTURES

The old tribal structures are still very important in rural areas. In the simplest unit of social structure, the nuclear family—father, mother, children—usually the man is its head. He has responsibilities not only within his own nuclear

A typical meeting between the elders and chiefs of a tribe.

and extended families—grandparents, aunts and uncles, cousins—but also in the village in which they all live—perhaps peacekeeping, organizing a festival, making sure spiritual observances are carried out, or looking after the water supply or sanitation. He forms part of the council of elders that advises the village chief on the running of the village.

In turn, the village chief sits on the council of elders of the divisional chief. A division might be a series of villages. Divisional chiefs advise the paramount chief, who is the highest authority in the clan. The paramount chief, like the lesser chiefs, inherits his position through his family, but he can be rejected by his people in favor of a relative if he turns out to be an ineffective leader. In the north of Ghana the chief's symbol of power is an animal skin, while in the south it is a stool.

When they become chief, they are "enstooled" or "enskinned," and if they are removed from office, they are "destooled" or "deskinned." Ordinary citizens can never become chief. Successive national governments have never sought to interfere with the chieftaincies. At the regional level, however, the paramount chiefs meet in a body set up by the government called the Regional House of Chiefs. Regional houses elect representatives to sit in a National House of Chiefs. When disputes between paramount chiefs occur, a judicial committee made up of chiefs and a high-court judge adjudicates.

Each paramount chief and his elders can make bylaws regarding traditional matters. They arbitrate on tribal matters, such as land tenure, inheritance, and custom. They are the essential core of all festivals that take place in Ghana. Although they have no legal role in local government matters, their disapproval of a new project or local government law would ensure that it did not happen. The paramount chiefs embody all that is best in their clans. On important occasions they wear beautiful ceremonial clothing and gold and silver jewelry.

THE FAMILY

The most common traditional family unit in Ghana is matrilineal, where a person is related to everyone on the mother's side of the family, including the mother's brothers, sisters, nieces, nephews, aunts, and uncles. In rural areas

An extended family in northern Ghana, living together in a compound.

the matrilineal family often lives in one compound or neighborhood and shares the land and property communally. Such an extended family would be called a clan. In Ghana it is known as an *abusa* (ah-BOO-sah).

Less common are patrilineal families, where the family or clan is made up of those on the father's side. Included in the unit are the spirits of dead family members. At the head of the clan is the chief, the man who sits with the village elders and carries out the tribal duties. In a small village all the residents may be from one family. When a chief is deposed or dies, all the sons of the women in his family of the next generation are potential candidates for his position. The mothers in the clan are thus important and powerful, especially the mother of the chief.

The clan system affects every aspect of the Ghanaian lifestyle. Land tenure is held by the family, so land is rarely sold. Every member of an *abusa* has equal rights to the resources of the clan; likewise, any individual's wealth belongs to their family. The clan system also affects how public works are carried out in villages. If a new well or schoolroom is needed, it will belong to the whole *abusa*. Everyone therefore lends a hand or, if they can, donates cash to the building project.

URBAN SOCIAL STRUCTURES

The clan system is less conspicuous in urban areas. Many people have migrated to the towns, leaving behind their traditional groups. They now earn salaries and live in nuclear families. If they are able to save, they will use the money to put their children through school or buy household goods or even their own house. Their lingering ties to the clan may be their general sense of duty or sentimental associations, rather than shared ownership of property. Nuclear family size is small.

MARRIAGE

The traditional Ghanaian concept of marriage is very different from the Western one. Arranging a marriage is one's father's responsibility; so when the son chooses his life partner, he tells his father about his choice. His mother usually checks the suitability of the girl. She might ask neighbors about illnesses in the family, and determine how closely related she is to her future husband.

This young bride and groom chose Western dress for their wedding.

If she is acceptable, the father begins negotiations. A cryptic message passes between the two fathers, and the girl's family members do their own check on the boy and his background. A message goes back if the boy is found acceptable, and the wedding plans begin. By this time the boy's father will have made two cash gifts to the bride's family—one when he sends his preliminary message, called the "knocking fee," and another when the agreement was accepted. A third payment is the "bride wealth" when the girl is handed over. It is seen as an evidence of matrimonial union.

The first two fees are negotiated by the bride's father and they become his, but the third fee is a "deposit" that must be handed back in the event of a divorce. Among some clans other payments go to brothers, aunts, and other relatives to compensate for their loss. Often—for example, among the Grusi-speaking tribes in northern Ghana—payments are made with an animal.

When a couple marries, many expenses are involved besides the "bride wealth" and the wedding party. The groom must give his wife-to-be gifts to bring to the marriage. These might be furniture (such as a chest of drawers), sets of clothing, shoes, perfume, and money. The wife also must bring her share of family possessions to the marriage.

She still has the belongings she was given at puberty, but to these she must add household utensils, such as buckets, pots, dishes, towels, and other small items, as well as food for the first week of their marriage.

These wedding gifts are exchanged before the union is finalized, and it is only on acceptance of them that the marriage goes ahead. If either partner fails to provide his or her proper share, the marriage can be cancelled.

The marriage ceremony itself, a meeting between the parents to formalize the relationship, may or may not include either bride or groom. Afterward, the bride is summoned to the groom's house along with her friends and relatives. At the groom's house are his relatives, friends, and musicians. A boisterous party takes place, and the girl then remains at her husband's house.

Guests dancing and celebrating at a wedding in Ghana.

Among some ethnic groups, particularly the matrilineal ones, the girl and her husband often return to live at her own family home. Such is the case among the Fanti, an Akan tribe. Among some groups polygamy is common. The Fulani, for example, often live in family units of a man and his several wives and their children. Some men may have two families in separate homes, with two sets of children, each living with their own mother's clan. Divorce is a matter of paying back to the groom's family the "bride wealth." Any goods that the husband gave to the wife's family need not be returned.

CHILDREN

The clan system has greatly influenced family size. If a clan were to be strong, the next generation had to be large. In the past each couple was encouraged to have as many children as possible. As many as 13 births was common for each woman, although many of the babies did not survive. Tribal wars and slave raids claimed more children, and many others died from diseases such as malaria and river-borne diseases. Malaria remains a threat to children in Ghana, taking one in every four children below the age of five each year. Nowadays, with land becoming scarcer, more children means a smaller share for each member of the clan. Tribal wars have ended, the infant mortality rate has declined, education is expensive, and family planning is available. Tribal thought, therefore, focuses less on having many children and more about providing better for a few.

Even so, children are still seen as an economic and social asset to the clan. In their work for the family they repay the costs of their birth and upbringing. Children fetch water, sweep the yard, tidy the house, wash clothing, and help on the farm. Girls have the toughest workload—helping out on the farm, doing housework, and cooking for the family. Boys are treated more casually, being allowed time to play. In poor families boys are expected to contribute to the family income. Besides using slingshots to fell birds, they might do some gardening for pay. The more enterprising boys might have a small business of their own at a market. If they can collect enough money, they can buy snacks and sell them at a profit. Children as young as six may scamper around at such jobs in the evening after school.

When children grow up, their obligation to their parents continues. If they have moved to the town, they are expected to send money home regularly. If they still live in the village, they must provide for their parents, including their funeral expenses.

THE LIVING ENVIRONMENT

The cities offer a variety of homes to suit different budgets. There are government housing projects as well as developments of privately owned houses that would not seem out of place in an American city. The home of a typical city dweller is likely to have electricity, plumbing, good sanitation, and consumer appliances such as a TV set, refrigerator, and perhaps even a VCR. Western-style upholstered armchairs and carpets may fill the rooms. The wealthiest people in Ghana have lifestyles that are comparable to those of their counterparts in the West.

Some districts of cities, such as Nima in Accra, are slums or shantytowns. Those areas escaped town planning and have no piped water, electricity, or sanitation. Often open sewers flow through the streets. In Accra some 700,000 people have no access to sanitation. Many of those who live in the shantytowns are poor migrants who have no clan system to support them, no financial resources, and no patches of land to grow their food. They mostly live from hand to mouth.

In the countryside the traditional house is built by its owner out of the cheapest available materials. No planning permits are required, nor are there rules about sanitation. A typical village house of someone who is fairly well-off has several rooms, including a kitchen, bathroom, living room, and verandah, where most of the day's activities take place.

Each parent may have their own bedroom, with shared rooms for young girls and individual rooms for teenage girls and each boy. Typical household furniture may include carved stools that are kept indoors, with some chairs and crude wooden stools outside. The bedrooms may have a simple wooden bed with a mattress and a sheet. Floors are covered in reed mats. Clothes and possessions are kept in chests. Children sleep on woven rush mats that are aired outdoors every day.

In the village one may find a communal well, an elementary school, a church or mosque, perhaps a bar or café, and a few public buildings such as a mill, a dispensary and clinic, and a marketplace. Beyond the village are the fields, where the crops are grown and animals grazed.

HEALTH

Some parts of Ghana experience long periods of either torrential rain with flooding or severe drought. Water management thus is an important aspect of the nation's health care. About half the rural population does not have access to safe drinking water. Many people draw their water from a nearby river, which may be polluted by insecticides, the runoff from a factory upstream, or sewage and animal waste. Where complex water systems have been installed, such as piped water from a well, the local community may not have the means or skills to maintain it and the supply is lost.

A nurse dispenses medication to her patients. Groups of medical teams often go out to care for the needs of the rural population in Ghana.

Most rural women in Ghana depend on traditional midwives for help in delivering their babies. Many local midwives nowadays have been trained in nutrition for expectant mothers as well as basic hygiene. Charities, the churches, and the government have also set up clinics in many villages, where vaccination programs are carried out and rudimentary health care is provided. For more serious illnesses, people must travel to urban areas, where most of the government hospitals are located.

Coming of age is an important part of life for village children. It marks their arrival at adulthood and is celebrated by the whole village. It is usually incorporated into one of the festivals observed by the village.

Boys from the Fanti ethnic culture are given the uniform of their local militia. (The militia, in addition to combating crime in their communities, engages in social and economic activities to help promote community development.) The night before the festival a bonfire is lit and the teenage boys to be initiated and their fathers gather together. They are taught the secret stories of their militia and purification rituals are carried out.

The Dipo puberty ceremony for girls of the Krobos group are more elaborate, with rituals varying according to the customs of the clan. Generally they follow the pattern that on reaching puberty, girls are taken to the family compound and put on display for all the neighbors to see. In other ethnic groups they walk around the streets, greeting the villagers. In some tribes the girls wear very little besides beads. After this there is an eight-day period when the girls are isolated and cannot touch anything associated with adult life, such as the stove, their newly bought clothes, or the gifts that their family and neighbors bring. At the end of this period of exclusion, the girls are dressed in their finest new clothes and are presented with gifts that form their capital and that remain their personal property even after marriage.

EDUCATION

Compared with many of its African neighbors, Ghana has a good educational system. At 4 years of age a child's educational journey begins with two years of kindergarten. All children between ages 6 and 12 attend six years of free and compulsory elementary education. In rural areas facilities can be as humble as a shady spot under a tree. Often teachers are difficult to recruit for poor and remote locations. They are usually relocated from another part of Ghana and are not part of the local clan, so they may feel excluded and find life quite hard. For the first three years, teaching is in the mother tongue and English is taught as a second language. Subsequently, English becomes the official medium of instruction.

Students learning English, an official language at school.

After elementary school those who can afford it go on to three years of junior secondary school (middle school) and a further four years of senior secondary (high school) level. Successful completion of senior secondary school leads to admission eligibility at training colleges, polytechnic institutions, and universities. Although Ghanaians value education highly, about 25 percent of children drop out after completing elementary school because their parents cannot afford the cost or the children must work to contribute to the family income. In rural Ghana many girls envision their future only in marriage and drop out of school at an early age. Many parents see little need for an expensive secondary education for a girl who will marry before age 20 and begin farming and child rearing.

In addition to the state educational system, there are a number of private schools. An important feature of the government's efforts to establish literacy in the country are mass education campaigns that make use of the radio to teach literacy, citizenship, health care, good farming practice, and house building.

Ghanaian children—like children worldwide—are fascinated by computers and are eager to learn how to use them.

RELIGION

The Cathedral of Our Lady of the Seven Sorrows, in the northern city of Navrongo, was built in 1906.

G HANA HAS MANY RELIGIOUS BELIEFS and customs and almost all Ghanaians practice one religion or another. It is a secular state, so the government does not favor or support any religion over another. The three main religions in Ghana are Christianity, Islam, and animism. Of these, animism is the indigenous religion, while Christianity and Islam have been introduced from afar.

A traditional Asafo Fanti shrine.

Many people practice both animism and one or another of the introduced religions, so statistics vary. About 69 percent of the population believed to be Christians—24.1 percent Pentecostal/Charismatic, 18.6 percent Protestant, 15.1 percent Catholic, and 11 percent other Christian churches. About 16 percent of the population is Muslim, with slightly less than half of those following the Ahmadhiyah branch of that belief, based on Shia practices. Generally more people in the north are Muslim, while more people in the south are Christian. The rest of the population practices traditional African beliefs, other religions, or none at all.

TRADITIONAL BELIEFS

Many religions are included in the term "animism" in Ghana. These religions share the common idea that there exists a spiritual world in which such inanimate things as trees, rocks, streams, or even the village well are imbued with life or spirit (animated) and are able to cause harm or bring good to people who come in contact with them. Consequently, all objects must be treated respectfully and appeased if necessary. They can also be called on for help, using a juju priest as an intermediary agent.

Most of Ghana's ethnic groups believe in three forms of spiritual power— the spirits of the things around them, the spirits of their ancestors, and a single god, Nyame, who created the world. The creator god is less important in the daily lives of the animist peoples than the other two. Ancestors are the most important aspect of one's spiritual life, and the recently deceased are the most powerful of all. If properly treated, the ancestors are benevolent. But they can be vengeful if they are slighted—for example, by an improperly conducted ritual.

JUJU PRIESTS (SPIRITUAL HEALERS)

A mixture of physician and priest, the juju priest mediates between his patients or believers and the spirits. Also known as the *abirifo* or *bayi okomfo*, his job is often hereditary, with the father passing his skills on to the son. Often the son will have given some sign of his inclination, perhaps by falling into a trance. The priest has a great assortment of natural herbs and remedies for all kinds of illnesses. Because he may believe that an illness is caused by some malevolent spirit, such as an irritated ancestor, part of his cure may be to appease that angry spirit and to wear a talisman as protection against it. He creates charms, potions, and incantations to protect his patients against evil spirits, curses, and other spiritual mishaps.

A talisman is made of items that are believed to hold magical power. Often they are made of animal bone or skin. The more powerful an object was in life, the more power it has to protect the victim, so often the talisman will be part of a tiger or some other powerful creature. To obtain help from the juju priest, the family and the suffering person must visit the priest, bringing gifts. The priest listens to their problems and then works his magic to the drumming, singing, and dancing of his assistant priests. The juju is well paid for his ministry.

A juju priest and his assistant offer libations to appease the spirits.

Like the ancient Greeks, Ghanaians believe in a lone creator god, called Nyame, as well as a pantheon of lesser gods. They also pray to their ancestors for blessings and guidance. Many of them have adopted Christianity, which they practice hand in hand with their other beliefs.

In the Ashanti religion the supreme deity is called Nyame. Beneath him are a pantheon of lesser gods embodied by the earth's physical features, such as the Tano River, Nyame's favorite son. Below them are even smaller gods or abosom *(ah-BOH-som)— objects of spiritual power or the power that it represents. While Nyame is so remote that he cannot be appealed to, the* abosom *are ready to help if appealed to in the right way. All over Ghana* abosom *houses exist where the* abosom *are worshiped and addressed as if they were elders of the clan. Inside an* abosom *house is a brass basin containing the essential elements of the* abosom*—perhaps some river mud, herbs, beads, shells, or other revered objects. The* abosom *can enter into the body of a priest if it so wishes.*

Good luck charms worn by a local Ghanaian.

The sick may seek out an *odunsini*, who is a spiritual herbalist with great knowledge of herbs and concoctions. The healer is trained to navigate the rituals necessary for obtaining the herbs without offending the gods.

The *bosomfo* or *okomfo* incorporates all the functions of the other healers while playing the role of attendant to the gods (represented in the form of a shrine). The Ashanti nation was formed by the priest Okomfo Anokye who was believed to have received the golden stool from the heavens.

The Muslim religious healers in Ghana are called *malams*. They create talismans that contain quotes from the Koran and other writings, and herbs. These talismans are supposed to protect the wearer against evil spirits, bad luck, and diseases.

AKAN BELIEFS

The Akan people, who make up the largest group in Ghana, believe that a person is made up of three distinct spiritual and physical elements. Each person inherits their physical being, called the *mogya* (MOG-yah), or blood, from their mother and their spiritual side, or *ntoro* (n-TORO) or *sunsum*, from the father, and *okra*, the soul, from Nyame, the creator god. This belongs to Nyame and returns to him after death. The Akan have their own calendar, which consists of nine cycles of 40 days each, called *adae* (AHD-ay). In each cycle there are two special days on which the tribe pays its respects to the spirits of the ancestors.

The Akan maintain the stools of past chiefs, believing that their spirits rest in the stools. So in each 40-day period one day is set aside to honor the chiefs. The stool room is usually a sacred place that only the chief and the priests of the ancestors can enter. In some tribes ordinary people are never allowed to see the stools, even when they are taken outside for purification rites. During the day of worship the stools are visited by the chief and his attendants and are given food and drink, and the chief retells the stories of the ancestors' brave deeds.

The Ashanti golden stool has religious, political, and historical significance in the shaping of the Ashanti (also called Asante) nation and the identity of Ghana. The War for Independence, which began on March 28, 1900, was instigated by Yaa Asantewaa, a queen mother who mobilized the Ashanti troops to lay siege to the British mission at Fort Kumasi for three months. The British governor, Lord Hodgson, had demanded that the Ashanti turn over to the British empire the golden stool that was the throne and a symbol of the Ashanti struggle for independence. To force out information on where the golden stool was hidden, children and their parents were bound and beaten by the British, who had to bring in several thousand troops and artilleries to break the siege. The British troops also plundered villages, confiscated their lands, and killed many people. Queen Yaa Asantewaa was exiled to the Seychelle Islands, while most of the captured chiefs became prisoners of war. Yaa Asantewaa died twenty years later in exile. Today the Seat of State that is used ceremonially by the president of Ghana takes the form of the Akan stool. It was first used in 1960 when Ghana became a republic.

A ceremonial staff, featuring a golden figure seated on the Ashanti golden stool, symbolic of a chief, at a festival in Kumasi.

THE SUPREME BEING

An Akan story tells how the supreme creator, Nyame, got into the sky. In the very earliest days the creator lived close to man, on the rooftops of the houses. One day he was passing some old women pounding fufu *(FOO-foo), a doughy mixture of cassava and plantains. The harder the women pounded, the farther Nyame bounced into the sky until eventually he reached the highest heavens and decided to stay there. But by then he was no longer close to the people that he created, so he had to call on the tallest things to talk to his people for him. That is how people learned to worship the high things, such as mountains and trees, which were close to Nyame and could easily carry messages yet farther up to him. When the Ashanti create altars to Nyame, it is always in the shape of a tree with a fetish figure sitting in it. When a drum maker or boatbuilder cuts down a tree to make his drum or boat, he always propitiates the tree because of its mighty power to intercede between him and the supreme being, Nyame.*

CHRISTIANITY

The first Christians to come to Ghana were the Portuguese, who introduced Roman Catholicism in the 15th century. They made little effort to convert the local people, so Christianity did not take root until the second half of the 19th century, when missionary societies began to set up churches and schools.

The Basel Missionary Society started missionary work in Ghana in 1828. The Wesleyan Methodists arrived in the 1830s, led by Thomas Birch Freeman. He was half-African and went to the Ashanti region to set up his mission. By 1843 the Wesleyans had 21 missions in Ghana, and in 1876 they founded the first secondary school in the country. Farther inland, Bremen missions were established east of the Volta, working with the Ewe people. That fellowship later became the modern Evangelical Presbyterian Church of Ghana.

In the early years of the 20th century, many Ghanaians were converted to Christianity because of the work of William Wade Harris, a Liberian who traveled across West Africa and whose teachings were so persuasive that he was deported from Côte d'Ivoire. Although he was an American Episcopalian missionary, he helped to convert thousands of people from animism to Methodism, Roman Catholicism, and Anglicanism. His followers in Ghana set up their own new church, called the Church of the Twelve Apostles. Other Christian churches in Ghana include the Presbyterian, Evangelical, Baptist, African Methodist, and Episcopal Zion churches.

A wood carving of *The Last Supper* at the Cathedral of Our Lady of the Seven Sorrows in Navrongo.

SPIRITUAL CHURCHES

The churches that arrived in Ghana in the 18th and 19th centuries appealed to people because of their similar ideas of a single creator god and also because of their efforts to educate local people. But the nonnative churches all lacked an African flavor, and over the years indigenous churches that mixed the belief in a forgiving savior with the high spirits and enthusiasm of African cultural life began to spring up all across West Africa.

One of those churches was the Church of the Lord, Aladura. That began among the Yoruba people of Nigeria and was based on the ideas of an American church, the Faith Tabernacle Church of Philadelphia, which practiced faith healing and the laying on of hands. In 1918 a horrendous worldwide influenza epidemic killed many people in West Africa, and a prayer group within the Anglican Church started to practice faith healing in an effort to save lives from the viral onslaught.

By the 1920s that sect had been forced out of the Anglican Church, but it had become very popular and spread from its home in Nigeria across West Africa, establishing a branch called the Christ Apostolic Church in Ghana. Later churches came to be called Aladura churches and practiced even more occult forms of Christianity, featuring prophets who claimed they could foretell the future, heal the sick, and even make amulets for protection, just as the juju priests did. Often these amulets included inscriptions from the Bible rather than fragments of animal bone. Prayer meetings are often very lively, with singing, African-style drumming and street processions.

In Ghana the most important days in the Christian calendar are Christmas and Good Friday.

ISLAM

Islam arrived in Ghana with Arab traders taking gold to Sudan, probably sometime around the 17th century. It is more popular among the peoples in northern Ghana, although there are clusters of Muslims throughout the country. Most Fulani, Mamprusi, Dagomba, and some Ashanti have become Muslims.

Islam originated in Arabia in the seventh century and follows the teachings of the Prophet Muhammad. Muslims believe in one God, in angels who bring the word of God to the people, and in the 28 prophets who received God's direct message. One of those prophets, they believe, was Jesus Christ. Other prophets are Abraham, David, Moses, and the writers of the New Testament, all figures that are part of Christianity. Muslims also believe in the final day of judgment, when they will hear the trumpet of the angel Asrafil. The main form of Islam practiced in Ghana is Sunni Islam, but there is another sect, called the Ahmadhiyah, a Shia faction considered heretical by most other Muslims, which has converts in southern Ghana. That sect recognizes another prophet after Mohammed, a man called Mirza Ghulam Ahmad, who lived in India and claimed to be the *mahdi* (MAH-dee), the figure who was to appear at the end of the world. He also claimed to be the reincarnation of Christ and of the Hindu god Krishna.

In Ghana the sect is represented by the Telemul Islam Ahmadhiyah Movement, which has its headquarters in Saltpond. A proselytizing sect, it runs several secondary schools and is happy to convert people to any form of Islam, not just its own.

The Mamprusi and Dagomba clans of northern Ghana believe in the ancestors' powers and also in an earth spirit, shrines to whom are in sacred places. Many of these people are also Muslim who believe in one God and angel messengers.

The 16th-century Banda Nkwanta Sudanese-style mosque in western Ghana.

LANGUAGE

A man selling newspapers along the busy roads of Accra.

GHANA HAS ABOUT 100 indigenous languages and dialects. In the south those languages tend to be either a form of Twi, Ewe, or Ga, while in the north Dagbane is spoken. The northern and southern languages are not mutually intelligible, so several lingua francas, languages that people must learn to be able to do business with diverse groups, have evolved in the country.

The most widely used lingua franca is English, which actually is the official language of Ghana and the medium of instruction in schools. In other areas, Hausa, a language from Nigeria, is used for intertribal communication. Most people speak their own mother tongue fluently, understand a few related languages, know a little of the local lingua franca, and would have learned some English in school, which tends to take the form of pidgin English in rural areas. In the cities English is widely spoken, and English-speaking visitors have little difficulty making themselves understood. English is used for all government business, in the business community, for most radio and television broadcasts, and in most publications.

A teenager chatting on her cell phone, a universal accessory nowadays.

AKAN LANGUAGES

An adult woman learning how to read.

Most of the people who live along the coast and in the southern regions of Ghana speak an Akan language, mainly Twi-Fanti dialects. The Twi-Fanti dialects are very close, and speakers of those dialects can communicate quite well. The vocabulary is the same in most dialects, with differences only in pronunciation and accent. That means that people from the south coast can understand other speakers living as far away as the Black Volta, Lake Volta, or the border with Côte d'Ivoire, although the language they speak may be called Ashanti, Fanti, Akuapem, or any one of tens of other names. Because each language or dialect has a written form, they remain separate languages.

GUAN LANGUAGES

The people in northern Ghana speak one of three forms of the Guan language—Mole-Dagbane, Grusi, and Gurma. None of those languages is spoken or understood in the south of the country, except by the few people from the north who have migrated south to Accra or one of the other coastal towns. Mole-Dagbane is the most widely spoken branch of the Guan language. It includes the dialects spoken in the Nankansi, Gurensi, Dagomba, Mamprusi, and Talensi-Kusasi regions. Those languages are not as mutually comprehended as the Twi-Fanti dialects. Neighboring groups understand one another, but groups that live any distance apart cannot. Because of that, Dagbane, the language spoken in the Dagomba region, has become a lingua franca. When northern speakers and southern speakers meet, however, they almost always communicate in English, which has become another lingua franca. Thus northern Ghanaians know their own language and usually the language of their nearest neighbors, as well as Dagbane as the northern lingua franca, and English as the national lingua franca.

WRITING SYSTEMS

All Ghanaian languages existed only in a spoken form until the missionaries arrived in West Africa. In order to bring the message of the Bible to the local people, missionaries set out to learn the local languages and devise a written script for them. Because many of the missionaries who learned and transcribed the languages were linguists, they often wrote the dialects in the orthography of linguistics—inventing symbols representing sounds. Thus all over Ghana today public signs and notices written in local languages have some characters that are not in the roman alphabet. Not all Ghanaian languages have a written system. Languages in which teaching materials are being developed for use in high schools and colleges and for use in the media are Akan, Dagaare-Wali, Dagbanli, Dangme, Ewe, Ga, Gonja, Kasem, and Nzema. Another important written language is Arabic. Most Muslim children attend a *makaranta* (Islamic school) where they learn to read and write Arabic.

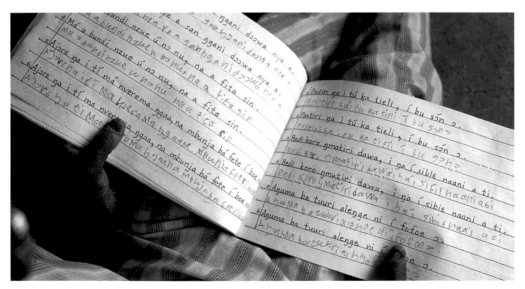

Thanks to the scholarly efforts of the missionaries, **Twi**, **Ashanti**, **Fanti**, **Ewe**, **Ga**, **Dagbane**, and many local languages have written forms today.

ENGLISH

A native speaker of English who arrives in Ghana and stands on the street listening may have considerable difficulty recognizing his own language being spoken. Not only is the accent different, the way words are strung together (syntax) is also different. Many African languages are tonal, meaning that the tone of the speaker's voice alters the meaning of the word, just as in Chinese dialects. Some Ghanaians have applied such a tonal system to English.

Another difficulty English speakers might encounter is unfamiliar vocabulary. In the United States and Britain some of the vocabulary has changed over the years, moving the two usages of English apart. That has happened in Ghana, too, where some older English words are still used together with new words from local languages or invented words. Other familiar English words have taken on new meanings.

For example, the word *dash* has joined the Ghanaian form of English and means *give*. Originally a Portuguese word, it has replaced *give* in local English.

The word *sister* is used more widely than in British English. In Ghana it can be used as a friendly form of address to any young woman; for example, school friends would call each other sister. Another expression is "my dear."

"NO ONE CAN DEVELOP THIS COUNTRY FOR US OTHER COUNTRIES CAN ONLY HELP US TO DO WHAT WE OURSELVES HAVE SET OUR MINDS TO DO"
FLT.-LT. J.J. RAWLINGS

This English billboard spurs the people of Ghana to constantly seek improvement in life.

> *Among many of the tribes of Ghana, an important member of the chief's entourage is the* okyeame *(otch-ee-AH-mee) or spokesman. He accompanies the chief on all his official duties and carries a special symbol of office, a mace. His job is to listen to what the chief says and translate it for the people, even if the chief and his people speak the same language. He spends his apprenticeship learning how to say things in the most euphemistic and flattering way.*
>
> *For everything that the chief wants to say, there is a polite and diplomatic way of saying it. The chief merely concentrates on the substance of his message, while the spokesman retells it for him in a literary and decorative way. The spokesman may not add any new information to the chief's words, but he can refer back to ancient stories or create a beautiful image. He polishes the chief's words for him. Among some tribes the spokesman also mediates between the chief and his subjects. The chief whispers to the spokesman what he wants to say and the spokesman makes the chief's words fit into a selection of well-known proverbs.*

In American English, it is a way of being friendly to someone. In Ghanaian English, it means girlfriend or boyfriend. Someone might therefore say, "I saw your my dear at church this morning," meaning "I saw your boyfriend." In British English, calling someone an "old crow" is a term of abuse, but in Ghanaian English it is a compliment, meaning that the person is wise and clever.

In some cases that form of English has become almost a new language, known as pidgin English, with not only its own vocabulary, but a different grammar system based on local languages. Often the verbs "is" or "have" are left out and the letter "s" is left off the ends of words. In other cases the word is repeated to make a plural. In many regions teachers find it easier to teach their pupils in the local pidgin version of English for the first few years and then move on to standard English in the senior years. Since many children do not go beyond elementary school, pidgin English is the only form they learn. Generally, the longer a student has been in school, the closer his or her English becomes to that understood and used in the United States or Britain.

PROVERBS AND STORIES

Much of Ghanaian folk wisdom is conveyed in a vast trove of proverbs that are well known to everyone in the country. The proverbs—moral tales that teach the values of the family and clan—are told to children again and again. They are often written or drawn on everyday objects. Mammy wagons (vans used for public transportation), for example, always have some message or drawing painted on the front. Sometimes such aphorisms as "The Lord is my shepherd" or "God is good," are taken from Christian or Muslim texts. More cryptic messages, written in English or a local language, might be "Poor no friend," meaning poverty is no friend to people. Both the van driver and his van are known by its slogan.

Moral tales include stories about the naughty spider Ananse. He is part human and part spider and is very wicked. He tries to cheat people, but always turns out to be too clever for his own good. The stories about him are fun to hear and teach children to be honest and well behaved.

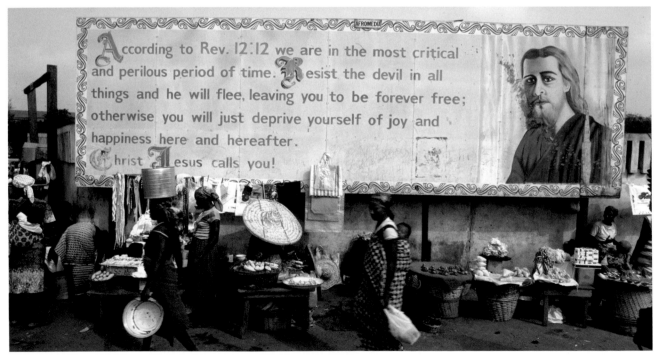

A religious sign in a busy market in Ghana.

TALKING DRUMS

Like many other countries in West Africa, Ghana has a tradition of talking drums. These are drums that are used as a means of communication rather than making music. They are hourglass-shaped, with skins stretched over both ends and joined by tightly drawn rawhide cords. As the cords are stretched or released by the drummer, the tone of the beaten drum changes, precisely following the tonal pattern of the language that it is copying.

In the days before telephones, the drummers of talking drums learned to beat out messages like a kind of Morse code, but the sounds that the drum made actually copied the sounds of the words they conveyed. Those drums are used today for ceremonial purposes, where once they relayed important messages across hundreds of miles.

NAMES

In southern Ghana people are named after the day on which they were born. This means that there are only 14 possible names: seven men's names—Kwajo (Monday), Kwabena, Kwaku, Yaw, Kofi, Kwame, and Kwesi—and seven women's names—Adjoa, Abena, Akua, Yaa, Efua, Ama, and Esi. Thus Kofi Annan was born on a Friday, while Kwame Nkrumah was born on a Saturday. In addition, each child is given a name chosen by his or her father, usually the name of a particularly respected ancestor. When two children in the same family are born on a same day, they will be given a number, too, so brothers both born on Friday will be called Kofi and Kofi Manu (second Kofi).

Other ways of naming a child might be to give a name that recalls some feature of their birth. An unexpected child born on Friday would be named Kofi Nyamekye (God given). A child born after the loss of a previous baby might be called Ababio (the returned one), meaning that the dead child has returned in the body of the new baby. In addition to those two names, there might be others, depending on the parents' wishes. Many people in the cities also take Christian names, so people have a minimum of three names and a maximum of ten or more. Children are not given the first names of their parents at all, so within a family everyone's names are completely different unless they were born on the same day!

ARTS

Dance, music, and drama are performed in the architecturally stunning National Theater of Ghana, in Accra.

A S IN MANY OTHER African cultures, in Ghana any distinction between leisure, art, religion, and festivals is a vague one. Ghanaian traditional arts and crafts evolved as a part of the religious and domestic needs of the people, while dance and music were, and still are, forms of worship and expressions of kinship. Those early art forms have slowly evolved into the music, art, and literature of present-day Ghana.

An art dealer standing amid the local paintings in her gallery.

A dilemma facing African writers is whether to write in their mother tongue or to write in the language of colonial times. The latter would take their work to a larger world audience, but carries with it painful echoes of the colonial past. On the other hand, writing in the mother tongue restricts most Ghanaian writers to an audience of no more than half their country's population.

MUSIC

Music is an integral part of Ghanaian life and culture. When a folk story is performed, it is usually accompanied by music, using either traditional instruments or more modern sounds. Music and singing accompany a Ghanaian's life from daily work to such major life events as birth, puberty, and funerals.

Most traditional music is played on four types of instruments—idiophones, such as rattles and xylophones, that would vibrate naturally; membranophones, such as drums; aerophones, such as horns and pipes; and chordophones, various types of stringed instruments.

The many musical instruments in Ghana have different uses within the various ethnic groups. Among some tribes their use is strictly restricted to particular religious events or may be played only for certain chiefs. The *nkofe* (n-KOFF-eh) horns may be played by the chief of the Ashanti clan, while the *kikaa* (KEE-kah) horn is used only in the Dagomba region and for praise songs about the divisional chiefs. Another example is the *apirede* (ap-eer-EH-deh) ensemble, made up of several drums, a gong, and clappers, which can be played only by the men whose job is to carry the royal stools of the chiefs.

Attendants blow tusk horns at an Ashanti festival.

Some drums are thought to imitate the cries of specific animals. One makes the ominous noise of a leopard, while another mimics a crocodile. They are played by tribes that regard those animals as totems.

One of the drums known as talking drums, the *atumpan* (at-UM-pan) of the Akan people, mimics the tonal language of the people. It is a sacred drum and can be made only by certain clan craftsmen. A drummer himself must never make his own drum. The drum is made from a specific tree, and the membrane is made from the ear of an elephant. The pegs that hold the membrane down are also made from a special tree. The variable tones of the drum are created by stretching or relaxing the pegs that hold down the membrane. The drum is played with a hammer often made from an elephant's tusk. This type of drum was once used to "telegraph" messages across great distances, but its use is more ceremonial and cultural today.

PALM WINE AND HIGHLIFE

The modern music of the Ashanti people is called palm wine. It is solo guitar music that originated in the small bars and drinking spots of southern Ghana. The singer plays an acoustic guitar and improvises songs on the spot about the customers or about politics. The songs are often uncomplimentary and can be hilarious.

Drummers playing the talking drums at a festival. In a drum ensemble, various drums are used in counterpoint to create varying rhythms, resembling speech.

Highlife originated in the port towns of southern Ghana in the 1920s and is a fusion of traditional drumming and European-style tunes. This kind of music gained international popularity in the 1950s after Ghanaian musicians such as E. T. Mensah discovered American jazz during World War II. Mensah formed a professional dance band like the big bands of 1940s America, but his style was uniquely African with powerful rhythms. In the 1950s many such bands in Ghana were popular.

Another important figure of the time was King Bruce, who played saxophone and trumpet and led the Black Beats, a band of some 20 musicians. He wrote songs in English and Ga. His career continued into the 1990s, and his songs were put onto CDs in 1997. Many more bands and individuals have found fame in Europe and the United States, notably Osibisa, Highlife International, Kantata, and Pat Thomas. The most popular highlife musician in the 1990s was Alex Konadu.

Since 2000, the Ghanaian music industry has organized a Ghanaian Music Awards to appreciate and reward musicians who have excelled in the five main music genres of Ghana: gospel, hip-life, highlife, reggae, and traditional.

Osibisa is one of the many Ghanaian bands that have found international fame.

DANCE

Like much in Ghanaian art, dance plays a large part in the lives of ordinary people. It is an ancient tradition and each movement of the dancer often expresses a symbolic as well as social meaning. The dances of the various ethnic groups are each different in style and in purpose. Particular movements are typical of the different clans. The Akans, for example, use complex footwork, coordinated with intricate hand and body movements. The dances of the Frafra are much simpler and are performed by columns of line dancers moving in synchronization and concentrating on foot stamping, with few hand or body movements except swaying.

Men dancing a fast-paced and acrobatic traditional north Ghanaian dance.

The Dagaba often incorporate stooping and leaping movements into their dances, while in northern Ghana the dances are more acrobatic, with tumbling and lifting. The dances of men and women also vary, with women's dancing being more sinuous and men's more angular and sharp. Individual movements convey symbolic meanings for the spectators. Reaching up to the sky indicates a call to God, while rolling the wrists together and drawing them sharply apart indicates the breaking of chains, or the freedom of the dancer. Mime often enters into the performances of the dances. Funeral dances are usually solemn and slow, while birth, puberty, and wedding dances are faster and more exhilarating.

ARTS AND CRAFTS

The most famous artifacts of Ghana are kente cloth and the gold weights and stools of the Ashanti chiefs. Among many groups cloth for clothing is a printed cotton, but among the Ashanti the cloth is woven in strips with intricate designs and is very valuable. Traditionally, kente cloth was woven only by men, although a few women have now learned the skill. In the 19th century weavers began buying silk thread from European traders and weaving it into the designs. The woven motifs are geometric and each weaver has his own style. The Ashanti chiefs have their own royal weavers, who make cloth for the chiefs and their mothers.

Each color and geometric design has its own meaning. Gold and yellow signify God, royalty, eternal life, and prosperity. White represents purity and joy, while green is newness and fertility. Red stands for death, so plain red outfits are worn at family funerals. Blue represents both love and the power of the queen mothers. Circles show the presence of God, triangles fertility and womanhood, and rectangles virility and manhood.

A local craftsman printing patterns on an *adinkra* cloth.

Adinkra is a main ceremonial cloth for most Ghanaians in the south. It has stamped patterns and symbols important to the Ghanaians and is worn for sad occasions. According to Ashanti legend, it was introduced in 1818 following the capture of a rival monarch, named Adinkra, who wore the cloth to express his sorrow on being taken to Kumasi. *Adinkra* designs are printed in a black dye made from the bark of certain trees, using stamps carved from sections of calabash wood.

COFFINS AS ART

Funerals are lavish and expensive affairs in Ghana, and the more important the deceased the more elaborate their funeral. In recent years an unusual art form has developed around the funerals of some Ghanaians, where coffin makers are commissioned to make a coffin that depicts the occupation of the deceased.

Thus a fisherman's coffin might be a huge tuna fish carved out of wood and painted, while a truck driver's coffin might be a small replica of the truck he drove. A pineapple farmer might be buried in a pineapple-shaped coffin, while a rich man might be buried in a model of a Cadillac automobile. People often commission their coffins long before they die since the work on each coffin is elaborate and may take many months of work. If the customer dies before his coffin is completed, the funeral is delayed until it is ready. Not surprisingly, these coffins are very expensive.

A collection of typical Ghanaian woven baskets, wooden carvings, metal sculptures, and clay pots.

Ancestral stools are another art form whose significance is far more than artistic in Ghanaian society. In some villages in central and southern Ghana, parents have a stool made for each of their children, and the stool comes to represent the child's life energy. People keep their own stool all their life, and when they die, their body is seated on the stool while it is prepared for burial. After death the stool is placed in the ancestral huts and is venerated by the family as the actual spirit of the deceased.

The stools are made of three pieces—a rectangular base, a seat that is curved like a barrel stave, and a carved supporting pillar or pillars between them, where the importance and character of the owner is described. For a wealthy chief or a rich man, the stool is intricately carved. In all cases the symbolism of the carvings is important. Some stools are plated with silver or, in the case of the early Ashanti kings, with gold. After death each person's stool is treated with egg yolk, soot, and sheep's blood, symbolizing peace and caution. Stool carvers are craftsmen and religious figures. When the wood for a stool is cut, religious rituals are performed.

Another art form that is also part of tribal religious beliefs is the carving of wooden figures. These may be kept in totem or fetish houses, where they either represent the animist gods or become intermediaries between the people and the animist gods. An infertile woman might carry a carved wooden doll on her back that would transmit her wish for children and may bring help from the animist spirits. Other such dolls may be placed around houses or on the outskirts of the village to protect the tribe. The dolls represent each tribe's vision of beauty and may be scarified or carved to represent the fertility of a woman or the angular qualities of men.

ARCHITECTURE

Ghana maintains an interesting architectural showcase of centuries-old castles and forts built by the Portuguese and British, modern buildings erected since the 1960s, and the indigenous building styles of the various ethnic groups.

Nothing remains of the city built by the Ashanti at Kumasi except some engravings. The last wars of the Ashanti against the British forces led to the sacking of the city. The engravings show complex structures built around central courtyards. Walls, doors, and shutters were intricately carved and, in the case of palaces, were covered in hammered silver or gold leaf. A royal pavilion has been reconstructed at the cultural center in Kumasi, showing what such a building would have been like.

Women decorating their mud huts. White clay is used to polish a mural pattern of broken calabash, handshake motifs, and crocodile reliefs.

Modern rural buildings are far more humble. In the south buildings are square, often built around a central courtyard, and have a corrugated iron roof. At the entrance to the compound is a loggia, or roofed gallery, where guests are greeted. The walls are made of dried mud and are constantly reconstructed and decorated by the women who live in the house.

In the villages of the north, a series of circular huts is built around a central courtyard. Roofs are pointed and thatched. In the far north roofs are terraced and form flat surfaces for drying crops or for the family to sleep during hot weather. The walls are clay or unfired earth and are decorated either with paint or designs etched into the drying mud. The buildings are often simple, with a kitchen area opening onto a courtyard and several sleeping rooms.

THE LOST-WAX PROCESS

The process was first noticed among the people of Benin, who used it to make large intricate bronze statues. The Ashanti used the technique when they made the gold weights that became part of the Ashanti chief's symbols of office. First a model of the weight is produced by building up a core made of loamy soil and water. After thorough drying, the core is covered with a layer of beeswax. The wax is carved and decorated with a bone tool. When the carving is complete, the whole object is covered in more layers of soil, and sticks are pushed through all three layers to hold the mold together. The mold is dried again with the wax completely sealed inside. A pit is dug and lined with charcoal, and the mold is fired until the wax melts and runs out. Then the empty space created by the melted wax is filled with molten gold. After the gold has cooled, the earth is scraped away from the outside and scooped from the core of the gold piece, revealing the decorated gold weight, seal, or amulet.

In the cities domestic architecture is Western in style. The bungalows of richer people have yards and a parking space for their car. Public housing consists of apartment buildings in various stages of modernity.

LITERATURE

The earliest form of literature in Ghana was the stories told over and over again by professional storytellers, who added to and updated the stories each time they were narrated. The stories would be told at special events, such as weddings, funerals, or other traditional ceremonies, and accompanied by guitar and percussion music and singing. Storytelling often formed the means by which the values of the extended family or clan were passed on to the next generation.

As tribal life gives way to modern city life, there is a fear that the old stories will be lost. Some of that oral tradition is being revitalized today, however, by performers such as Koo Nimo (Daniel Amponsah), who broadcasts modern versions of the ancient stories on Ghanaian radio. He maintains the moral and cultural aspects of the stories he tells, but like his predecessors, he updates the stories to bring in modern politics and issues.

Symbolism is an important part of the lives of Ghanaians. It can be seen in the design of kente cloth, in the patterns on the walls of huts, and in many other art forms. The chief's garments and jewelry are not just adornments. Each piece depicts a story of the chief's origins, his wealth, and the history of the clan. These symbols can be seen in other artifacts of Ghanaian life, such as on canoes, mammy wagons, ornamental gourds, stools, and cooking utensils.

A chameleon symbolizes a mixture of slowness and quickness as well as the impermanence of words, which can change just like the chameleon's colors. A snail and a tortoise together symbolize the desire for peace, since neither of those creatures is ever hunted or shot at. A human figure holding its ear and pointing to its eye indicates that blindness does not prevent understanding in other ways. All of these symbols carved onto domestic items remind the owners of popular Ghanaian proverbs that express maxims to live by with propriety and laughter.

Today many Ghanaian writers have gained recognition as novelists, poets, and playwrights. Some successful Ghanaian writers are Christina Ama Ata Aidoo, K. A. Bediako, George Awoonor-Williams, and Ayi Kwei Armah, who wrote the powerful novel *The Beautiful Ones Are Not Yet Born*, about life in a newly independent African country. Christina Ama Ata Aidoo is one of a small number of female African writers and has written *The Dilemma of a Ghost* and *Anowa*.

LEISURE

A mother and child enjoying a relaxing dip in a pool near a beach.

GHANAIANS LOVE MUSIC, dancing, and good company. In the villages all those ingredients come happily together in the many festivals and clan events that fill the calendar, especially in the period following the yam harvest. In the cities the tribal and family structures have given way to a more urban lifestyle, and nuclear families spend their leisure in the churches, markets, restaurants, bars, and clubs common in larger towns and cities.

Children playing *oware*, a traditional game using stones and chiseled cups.

Young and old Ghanaians alike enjoy watching soccer matches on television.

Ghanaians are essentially gregarious and outgoing people who welcome strangers to their homes and love giving and receiving gifts.

LEISURE IN THE CITIES

Most of the larger cities are in the south of Ghana, where the tourism industry is based. Accra has a flourishing nightlife, with many bars and music clubs that offer live music. A typical form of entertainment in the city is a concert party, which includes a play, a stand-up comic act, and music, while the audience drinks *akpeteshe* (ak-pet-ESH-ee), distilled palm wine. Ghana is the home of highlife music, an African big band sound that uses Western instruments and traditional drumming to produce African rhythms. In the large cities that hybrid music is enjoyed at concert parties and in the churches, where a form of gospel highlife has developed.

Accra has nearly 50 churches in its city center alone. Churches are the heart of social life for many people, and on Sundays music and joyous singing can be heard in many of them, especially the indigenous African ones. Other favorite meeting places include food stalls and "chop houses," inexpensive café-style places found all around the cities. European and Asian restaurants are also found in the city centers. Movie theaters are popular, with African and Western films vying for popularity with kung fu movies. Ghana has a National Theater, where local patrons and tourists can enjoy cultural shows and contemporary theater productions.

LEISURE IN THE COUNTRY

In rural areas leisure often takes second place to the grueling demands of the farming year. Leisure is more closely related to the festivals and traditions of the African religions than to the spare time or available cash of the people who live in the villages. Because so many rural people live at a subsistence level, leisure is found only in activities that also benefit the family group. If they find spare time after the harvest or early in the season while the crops are growing, men will go out and hunt small animals.

In the countryside many villages do not yet have a permanent supply of electricity, so events such as concert parties and movies are not common. There are, however, many traveling movie theaters that tour the villages, carrying their own generators and showing videos and movies. Where there are no clubs, bars, or spare cash, young people gather in village squares at sunset and sing together or play games well into the night. Many villagers have battery-powered radios, but in most small towns there are loudspeaker systems broadcasting radio programs in the streets.

Boys enjoying a Foosball game (table soccer) at a beach in western Ghana.

VISITING

Ghanaians enjoy visiting one another's homes. Greetings are very important among them, and even strangers will greet one another in the street. Usually the person in movement begins the greeting, so when people visit a home it is their job to begin. The host welcomes his guests with the word *akwaba* (ak-WAH-bah). The guests bring a modest gift of food or even money that will be left discreetly with the woman of the house. The guests are greeted at the entrance, or loggia, of the house and hands are shaken all around. They are then taken inside and seated. A glass of water is offered, and it is impolite to refuse. Then the host asks the guests why they have come.

That is a tradition known as *amanee* (ah-MAH-nee). The family listens while the guests give an account of their journey and reason for coming. Then the host gives a brief recital of recent events in his family, after which he stands again and repeats his welcome. The handshakes are repeated. When that formal part of the visit is finished, everyone relaxes and chats away with a drink of palm wine.

Ghanaian children playing soccer at Kaladan Park in Tamale.

SPORTS AND GAMES

By far the most popular sport in Ghana is soccer. Other favorites are boxing, Ping-Pong, hockey, basketball, cricket, and track and field. Ghanaians also play a game similar to cricket called *apaat* (ap-AHT). *Ampe* (AHM-pay), which involves jumping and clapping, is a popular game among Ghanaian girls.

Children love to play make-believe, accompanied by songs. Girls usually play apart from boys, but sometimes the children's games bring them together. Traditional games include one similar to checkers; boys' marbles games; and *oware* (oh-WAR-eh), a version of mancala, similar to backgammon, that is played sitting on the ground with a board with small bowls chiseled in it and seeds or pebbles.

Players in Obuasi prepping for a game of cricket, a ball and bat sport introduced by the colonial English.

BUYING AND SELLING

Buying and selling in the village market is a long, drawn-out but quite enjoyable process involving much chatting and prolonged bargaining. Buyers mention an item they wish to buy, and the vendor points out the high quality of the item, cost of production, difficulties in transportation, and so on and on, and names a price. The buyers pretend to be shocked at hearing the price, and so the negotiations begin. When the sale is completed, the buyers may ask for extras. If vegetables were bought, the extras might be salt or cooking spices, or a couple of smaller vegetables to go with the main purchase. The more produce that has been bought, the more the buyer can expect as extras.

In the city the same process of bargaining takes place over wares in the markets, although extras are usually included only with foodstuffs. In department stores prices are fixed. Just as in the rest of the world, shopping in department stores or even in markets is often a leisure activity.

FESTIVALS

A performer plays traditional drums during a festival in Ghana.

Over a hundred festivals are celebrated in Ghana. Most of them predate Christianity or Islam and have their origins in the animist religions that are indigenous to Ghana. They largely follow the cycle of the seasons, with harvest festivals being the major events celebrated across the country. Most regions have rustic festivals that exalt the first yam harvests or the end of the harvesting season.

Tribal festivals remain an important part of modern Ghanaian life.

Other celebrations commemorate the arrival of the clan into Ghana or offer remembrance to the ancestors. Some mark a new start in the year and involve ritual cleaning of the house or clearing of the land around the village. Originally religious in nature, the activities reaffirmed the group's belief in the spirit world. Today, however, they are more culturally oriented. Celebrations center around the tribal chief—the custodian of the clan's traditions. He has advisers who help him determine the correct date for a festival and the way it should be celebrated.

Merrymakers dress up in fanciful masks during a festival in Ghana.

In the past urban people were allowed time off from work to return to their ancestral lands to celebrate important festivals. Families would stand at the edge of the village waiting for their relatives in order to escort them home with much music and singing. Anyone who did not take part in the ceremonies could be fined. This rule has been relaxed, as many people now live in the cities and contact with the home village has become less frequent. Nevertheless, the festivals are still a time for returning home if possible, for settling old feuds and land disputes, and for having a very good time. All festivals, even the somber ones, involve a great deal of dancing, singing, feasting, and drinking.

ODWIRA

Odwira, meaning purification, is the festival at which the new harvest of yams is presented to the ancestors and rituals are performed to purify the town. This event is celebrated particularly among the Akan people, as well as

DURBARS

The highlight of every festival is the durbar, a kind of pageant, in which the chief of the clan is dressed in his finest clothes and seated on a palanquin, a chair carried by several of his servants. He is shielded from the heat of the sun by a large and colorful umbrella. The lower chieftains follow in the procession, also adorned in their best clothes. The chiefs are carried to the place where the festival is to take place and their attendants—the executioners of older times—tell stories of past triumphs in battle. Each lesser chief goes before the regional chief to offer his allegiance, taking off his crown and one shoe and bowing before him. The regional chief then makes a welcoming speech to his people, and the festival gets under way.

in Akim, Akuapem, Akwamu, and also other states though under different names. The celebration itself lasts about a week, but ritual preparations last through an entire *adae* of 40 days. It usually takes place in September or October, depending on the harvest. Any eating of new yams is prohibited until the festival is over. For 40 days before the festival, all singing, dancing, and noise in the village are banned. Even funerals, which are usually noisy affairs, must be quiet. Seven days

A local chief is carried in a palanquin chair at the Odwira festival.

before the festival the path to the mausoleum of the past chiefs is swept. Six days before, tubers of the new yam harvest are paraded through the streets. A procession goes to the mausoleum with a sheep and rum to feed the spirits of their ancestors. The procession returns to the chief, and a blessing and purification ritual takes place. Drummers triumphantly play all through the night.

On the fifth day before the festival the village grows silent, and all the local villagers fast and remember their dead ancestors. Everyone wears brown clothes and red turbans to commemorate the dead. On the fourth day before, a huge feast is held for both the living and the dead. Unsalted cooked yam and chicken are taken in procession and laid at a shrine on the outskirts of town. The food for the dead chiefs is placed at the head of the procession, shaded by huge, colorful umbrellas. In every home food is laid out for everyone to eat, and there is a main feast in the center of the village. That night there is another ceremony, now accompanied by drumming and singing. Most people stay inside their homes as the dead chiefs' stools are paraded through the town to a stream for their annual ceremonial cleansing. Only privileged persons are allowed to see the cherished stools. On the day of the festival is the great durbar, where all the neighboring chiefs arrive to show their respect and pledge their allegiance to the regional chief. They are paraded through the streets of the town, carried on palanquins and accompanied by drummers and servants bearing gold swords and guns. Then the chiefs settle down together in the central square, and dancing and singing performances take place. Drinks and food are offered, and the local chiefs reaffirm their loyalty to the regional chief.

Dancers perform a ritualized enstoolment during Odwira in Kumasi.

The various clans of the Akan all celebrate different versions of the Odwira festival, but the essential elements are the same—the dead are remembered and thanked for the new yam harvest, the village is purified, the chiefs take part in the durbar, and a great feast is held.

OTHER FESTIVALS

THE AYERYE This is a Fanti festival in which each newly mature young man of the tribe is initiated into the clan of his father. A boy is a member of his mother's clan until puberty, when he is officially inducted into his father's militia. The festival takes place between September and December, usually to coincide with the harvest festival.

THE ABOAKYIR (DEER HUNT) FESTIVAL In Winneba a 300-year-old festival is held in which two competing teams hunt deer. The winning team is the first one to bring back the game. The trick is that the deer must be brought down with only sticks and cudgels. The festival usually takes place in May.

THE HOMOWO FESTIVAL Among the people of the Ga traditional area in the Greater Accra Region there is a monthlong thanksgiving festival that means "hooting at hunger." It originated from a period of great famine that was followed by a bumper harvest of grain and fish. Visitors are invited into village homes to join in the feasting.

An antelope is caught by hand and offered to the chief at the Aboakyir festival in Winneba.

THE PATH CLEARING FESTIVAL This festival dates back to the time before modern roads, when it was the duty of each citizen of the village to return home once a year and help clear the village paths, particularly those leading to the shrines and the village well. It is an Akan festival, practiced by the Gomua and Agona tribes.

Nowadays there may be no paths to clear at all, but the festival is still a good reason for families to return home and have some fun together. The festival usually takes place just before the new yams are presented to the ancestors.

FOOD

A fish market in Accra. In Ghana fish
is more commonly eaten than meat.

»❙N SOME AREAS OF GHANA, especially in the north where weather conditions can be extreme, hunger often poses a serious problem for as long as half a year. In the north food is harvested during a long dry season that follows a wet season that has been at times too short for the growing crops. That is followed by another period in which new crops are sown, when heavy manual energy is needed to look after the fields.

In the south the climate is less harsh. There are cities where food can be stored more efficiently, and most people have money enough to buy their food. In the east there is very fertile soil, abundant rainfall, and a mild climate, and large farms produce both cash crops and staples that are transported to the cities.

STAPLES

Staples are the foods that make up the bulk of a person's diet. In the West that is often wheat, potatoes, or to a lesser extent, rice. In Ghana the staple

Markets in Ghana are hives of activity, with many different types of vegetables and fruit bought and sold each day.

foods vary according to the region. In the north millet (a grain), yams, and corn are the staple foods, while in the south and west, plantains, cassava, and cocoyams (taro) are grown. Across to the southeast, which is drier, corn and cassava are the staple foods.

In the center of the country there are also areas where rice is grown and makes up part of the local diet. Both hill rice and wet rice are grown and eaten in Ghana. Rice is a practical foodstuff because it is easy to store.

Canned foods and other essentials can be found at a convenience store in the Makola market in Accra.

Cocoyam grows in the forest regions of Ghana. It is a low-growing plant and needs warm, damp soil. Some cocoyam plants are harvested for the shoots, while others are collected for the roots. An indigenous plant, it grows wild throughout the forested region, but it is also cultivated.

Cassava is a root vegetable that grows in a wide range of conditions, with some species tolerating the dry climate of the north, and others preferring the wet forest belt. It is rendered by a complex process into flour. In its raw state cassava contains a form of cyanide and, if not processed properly, is poisonous. The tubers can be left in the soil until they are needed, and cassava is often the last food staple left at the end of the dry season. Corn and millet are grains that grow in full sun and can tolerate fairly dry conditions. Both the grain and flour are cooked.

MEAT AND FISH

Meat is a rare luxury in many Ghanaians' diet. In rural areas animals that can be seen and counted by others represent wealth and so are rarely slaughtered. They provide a form of currency and are often used as dowry payments or are bartered at the market for imported goods. When meat does appear in meals it is usually as an ingredient in a stew rather than as the main dish. Fish and chicken are more common and often appear in stew.

OTHER FOODS

Groundnuts (peanuts) are an important source of protein and are grown mostly in the north. Palm nuts form the basis of most soups and stews. Green vegetables include the leaves of the cocoyam, known as *kontomire* (kon-toh-MEER-eh), a form of spinach, and okra, as well as eggplants, onions, tomatoes, sweet potatoes, and many kinds of beans. There are also several vegetables that grow only in specific areas of Ghana and are unknown in other parts.

THE KITCHEN

The traditional kitchen in rural houses contains a wood-burning open hearth that is recoated every day in fresh white clay. Standing in the hearth is a tripod for holding the stewpot, while fresh wood is stacked up at the side, ready for use. There is also a covered stove, fueled by charcoal, which is used for faster cooking, such as frying. Assorted pots and pans are stored in a chest. Those often include a big cauldron for cooking stews and a large iron griddle for frying. Out in the yard would be two mortars and pestles—one for crushing small nuts and grains and a larger one for pounding cassava and plantains to make *fufu* or *kenkey*.

Women pounding cassava and plantain to make *fufu*, readying for a meal.

DAILY MEALS

Usually three meals a day are eaten. In the countryside where there is much work to be done, the midday meal might be only a snack and the breakfast a more substantial meal. In the home the family separates at mealtimes. The men eat their food from one bowl, taking turns to help themselves with their right hands only. The women and girls share another bowl of food, while the boys eat together. There are well-practiced rules about who eats the meat or fish first and how it is to be shared.

The most commonly eaten evening dish in Ghana is *fufu*, a dough made from a mixture of cooked cassava and either plantain or cocoyam. It is served with a soup that might be made from a mix of groundnuts, palm fruit, fish, beans, or other vegetables, all simmered for an hour. The soups that include groundnuts are usually thick and grainy, while those made with palm fruit have a thick, yellow, oily texture. Other stews have special names—*forowe* (foh-ROH-weh) is a fish stew with tomatoes, while *nkatekwan* (en-KATI-ku-an) is a chicken and peanut stew.

Chilies are commonly grown and used in Ghanaian cooking, and a favorite soup is pepper soup, which is hot and peppery.

A popular breakfast dish called *ampesi* (am-PEH-si) consists of cassava, cocoyam, yam, and plantain mixed together, boiled, pounded to break up the fibers, and then boiled again with onion and fish.

Another common base for a meal is *kenkey* (ken-KAY), which is made from cornmeal. The meal is ground and soaked in water and left to ferment for two days. Then the mash is formed into balls and dropped into boiling water.

A woman prepares *krako*, a favorite on the street, for a snack.

After an hour the pasty mash balls are wrapped in plantain leaf packages and kept for two days. They are eaten with a spicy sauce with fish or stew as a substitute for *fufu*. Similar fermented dough is made from cornmeal or millet in the north of the country. The Ewe make a version from corn dough and cassava mash.

SWEET DISHES

There are many sweet dishes in Ghana. Surprisingly though, not many of them are made from chocolate, despite the fact that chocolate is cheap and of very good quality in Ghana. Some sweet dishes are built around the staple starchy vegetables. One popular dish is *tartare* (TAR-tar), or pancakes made from ripe plantain, pounded and deep-fried in palm oil. Mixed with corn flour and made into balls like doughnut "holes," plantain becomes *krako* (KRAHkoe). With boiled soybeans added, it becomes *aboboe* (ah-BO-bo-ee). Sweet dishes are not served as desserts after the main course, but are eaten as snacks at any time of the day.

EATING OUT

As Ghana has a growing tourist industry there are many restaurants that cater both to foreigners and to wealthier Ghanaians, especially in towns along the southern coast. Foreign cuisine, especially European-style, Indian, and Chinese, is common. Less expensive are the chop houses, which are casual cafés selling local food. The cheapest way of eating out is at a street stall, usually run by a woman, selling rice with various toppings. A popular street snack is *kelewele* (ke-leh-WEH-leh), or fried plantains seasoned with ginger and chili. *Koko* (KO-ko) is corn or millet porridge mixed with milk and sugar. Other stalls sell slices of fresh fruit or coconuts that are slashed open on the spot for the customer to enjoy the water and meat.

Pito, a beer made from millet, is a popular beverage in Ghana.

DRINKS

As readily available in Ghana as in the rest of the world are the ubiquitous cola drinks. Ghana produces some soft drinks of its own, such as Refresh, a fizzy soda made with fresh fruit juice, and Supermalt, a dark-colored nonalcoholic drink tasting of malt. Beer is very popular. Ghana was the first West African country to have a brewery. There are several local beers nowadays as well as imported beers. More unusual drinks include iced *kenkey*, which is the northern fermented corn flour dissolved in water and fermented further. Another unusual taste more common in the north is *pito* (PEE-toh) beer, made from millet rather than hops. In the south the drink of choice is palm wine, which can range from very alcoholic to nearly nonalcoholic.

NKATEKWAN (CHICKEN PEANUT STEW)

4 servings

1 3-lb (1.5-kg) chicken, cut into serving pieces

1 teaspoon (5 ml) salt

1 onion, chopped

1 tablespoon (15 ml) grated fresh ginger

2 cups (500 ml) water

½ cup (125 ml) smooth natural-style
   peanut butter

2 tablespoons (30 ml) tomato paste

2 cups (500 ml) fat-free low-sodium chicken
   broth

2 tomatoes, chopped

1 medium sweet potato, peeled and cut into
   1-inch (2.5-cm) cubes

2 cups (500 ml) fresh or frozen okra (optional)

1 teaspoon (5 ml) crushed red chili pepper

1 teaspoon (5 ml) dried thyme

- Discard visible fat and rinse chicken pieces in water.
- In a pot over medium heat, combine chicken, salt, onion, ginger, and two cups (500 ml) of water.
- Bring to a boil; reduce heat, and simmer for about 15 minutes.
- In a small bowl blend peanut butter with one-half cup (125 ml) of liquid from the pot. Stir mixture into pot.
- Blend in tomato paste, add broth and remaining ingredients.
- Bring to a boil. Reduce heat, cover, and cook until done, about 25 to 30 minutes.

ACCRA BANANA PEANUT CAKE

8 servings

1 ¼ cup (300 ml) butter, softened

2 cups (500 ml) sugar

4 eggs, beaten

4 ¼ cups (500 g) flour

1 teaspoon (5 ml) salt

4 teaspoons (20 ml) baking powder

½ teaspoon (2.5 ml) baking soda

8 bananas, mashed

½ cup (125 ml) unsalted peanuts,
    coarsely chopped

½ cup (125 ml) sugar (for sprinkling)

1 teaspoon (5 ml) ground cinnamon

- In a large bowl, cream together the butter and sugar. Add the eggs a little at a time and beat to combine.
- In a separate bowl, stir together the flour, salt, baking powder, and baking soda.
- Stir the flour mixture into the butter mixture alternately with the bananas and peanuts.
- Pour the batter into a lightly greased 9-inch cake pan and bake at 350°F (180°C) for 30 minutes, or until a wooden toothpick inserted in the center comes out clean.
- Remove from the oven and allow to cool on a wire rack.
- Sieve together the half cup (125 ml) sugar and cinnamon powder. Sprinkle this mixture over the top of the cake as soon as you remove it from the oven.

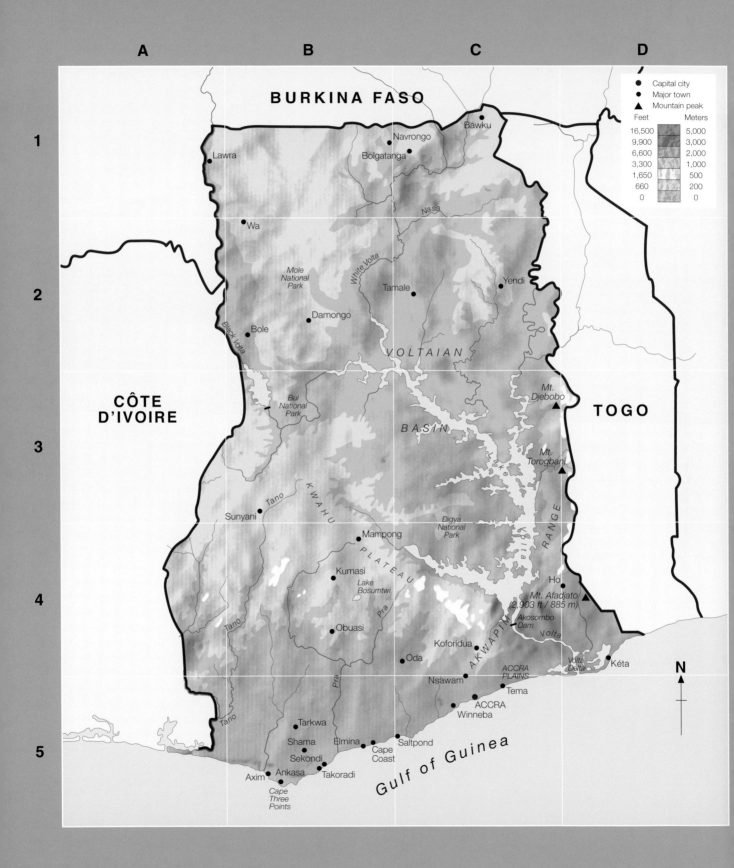

MAP OF GHANA

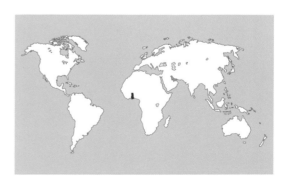

ECONOMIC GHANA

Services
 Airports

 Ports

 Tourism

Manufacturing
 Chemicals

 Food and beverages

 Furniture

 Textiles

Agriculture
 Cacao

 Cashew nuts

 Cola nuts

 Cotton

 Palm

 Shea nuts

 Timber

 Tobacco

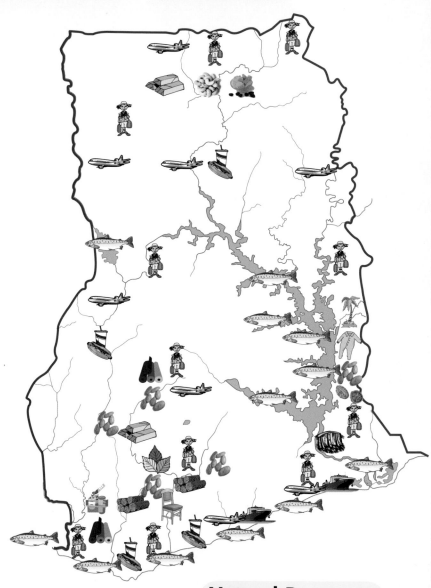

Natural Resources
 Fishing

 Gold

 Hydroelectric power

ABOUT THE ECONOMY

OVERVIEW

Ghana is well endowed with natural resources of gold and is a world producer of cacao. Most Ghanaians, 56 percent of the population, are employed in agriculture. Gold, cacao, and timber are major sources of foreign exchange. Ghanaians aspire to achieve economic success by creating a favorable business environment. With some international financial aid and technical assistance, Ghana may one day soon realize its vision, given the tenacity of its people to succeed.

GROSS DOMESTIC PRODUCT (GDP)

$34.04 billion (2008 estimate)

GDP GROWTH

6.3 percent (2008 estimate)

INFLATION RATE

16.4 percent (2008 estimate)

POPULATION BELOW POVERTY LINE

28.5 percent (2007 estimate)

CURRENCY

The cedi (GHS)
1 cedi (GHS) = 100 pesewas (Gp 100)
Notes: GH¢ 1, 5, 10, 20, and 50
Coins: Gp 1, 5, 10, 20, 50, and 1
USD 1 = 1.5 cedis (2009 estimate)

LABOR FORCE

11.52 million (2008 estimate)

UNEMPLOYMENT RATE

20 percent (2008 estimate)

AGRICULTURAL PRODUCTS

Cacao, rice, cassava (tapioca), peanuts, corn, shea nuts, bananas, and timber

NATURAL RESOURCES

Gold, timber, industrial diamonds, bauxite, manganese, fish, rubber, hydropower, salt, petroleum, silver, limestone

MAIN INDUSTRIES

Mining, lumbering, light manufacturing, aluminum smelting, food processing, cement, small commercial ship building

MAIN EXPORTS

Gold, cacao, timber, tuna, bauxite, aluminum, manganese ore, diamonds, horticulture

MAIN IMPORTS

Capital equipment, petroleum, foodstuffs

MAIN TRADE PARTNERS

Export partners: Netherlands 11 percent, United Kingdom 9 percent, France 6.2 percent, United States 5.9 percent, Germany 4.6 percent, Belgium 4.4 percent

Import partners: Nigeria 15.1 percent, China 14.9 percent, United Kingdom 5.2 percent, United States 5.1 percent (2007 estimate)

CULTURAL GHANA

Navrongo Cathedral
Built in 1906 and originally called Our Lady of Seven Sorrows, this traditionally built structure was painstakingly constructed and decorated by the locals, and is also the last remaining mud cathedral in Ghana.

Wechiau Hippo Sanctuary
This 25-mile (40-km) -long and 1-mile (2-km) -wide sanctuary in Wa stretches down the length of the Black Volta River, and is home to various species of mammals and reptiles. Besides the many hiking trails to explore, hikers can also spend the night in jungle treehouses and experience one of the best dawn choruses (bird song) in all of Africa.

Larabanga Mosque
Considered one of the most endangered monuments worldwide, this 13th-century historic Sudanese mosque in Tamale is one of the holiest sites in Ghana. An ancient Koran believed to have descended from heaven is still preserved in this architecturally marvelous mosque.

Boabeng-Fiema Monkey Sanctuary
This unique sanctuary in Kumasi is the only place where two different species of monkeys, the Campbell's Mona and the Geoffroy's Columbus, live harmoniously together alongside human beings. Regarded as sacred, protected by the law, and given proper funerals, these monkeys are part of society and local culture has been fashioned to include their acceptance.

Kakum National Park
Located in Elmina, Africa's only canopy walkway is suspended 100 feet (30.5 m) from the ground, offering a spectacular view from the tallest trees and a colorful array of patterns as the tropical birds glide through the lush greenery of the rain forest below.

Cape Coast Castle
This fortified castle and UNESCO heritage site was originally built by the Swedes in 1653 for the gold trade. Later seized by the Danes and then conquered by the British, the castle was used as a main slave-trading fort during the trans-Atlantic slave trade.

Kwame Nkrumah National Park
Located in the main commercial area in Accra, the structures in this park provide interesting symbolic interpretations of the life and works of Dr. Nkrumah, widely regarded as the "founding father" of Ghana.

Akosombo Dam
The construction of this hydroelectric dam in the Akosombo gorge flooded the Volta River Basin and subsequently created Lake Volta, the world's largest man-made lake.

ABOUT THE CULTURE

OFFICIAL NAME
Republic of Ghana

LAND AREA
92,098 square miles (238,533 sq km)

CAPITAL
Accra

ADMINISTRATIVE DIVISIONS
Ashanti, Brong-Ahafo, Central, Eastern, Greater Accra, Northern, Upper East, Upper West, Volta, Western

HIGHEST POINT
Mount Afadjato (1,040 feet/880 m)

POPULATION
23,832,495 (July 2009 estimate)

LIFE EXPECTANCY
Total population: 59.9 years (2009 estimate)
Male: 58.9 years
Female: 60.7 years (2009 est.)

LITERACY RATE
57.9 percent

BIRTHRATE
28.6 births per 1,000 population (2009 estimate)

ETHNIC GROUPS
Akan 45.3 percent; Mole-Dagmani 15.2 percent; Ewe 11.7 percent; Ga-Dangme 7.3 percent; Guan 4 percent; Gurma 3.6 percent; Grusi 2.6 percent; Mande-Busanga 1 percent; other tribes 1.4 percent; other 7.8 percent (2000 census)

RELIGION
Christianity 68.8 percent, Islam 15.9 percent, traditional African beliefs 8.5 percent, other 0.7 percent, none 6.1 percent (2000 census)

LANGUAGES
Ashanti 14.8 percent, Ewe 12.7 percent, Fanti 9.9 percent, Boron (Brong) 4.6 percent, Dagomba 4.3 percent, Dangme 4.3 percent, Dagarte (Dagaba) 3.7 percent, Akyem 3.4 percent, Ga 3.4 percent, Akuapem 2.9 percent, other 36.1 percent—includes English (official) (2000 census)

NATIONAL HOLIDAYS
New Year (January 1); Independence Day (March 6); Good Friday (variable); Easter (variable); Labor Day (May 1); Africa Day (May 25); Republic Day (July 1); Eid al Fitr or End of Ramadan (variable); National Farmers' Day (first Friday of December, hence variable); Eid al Adha or Feast of the Sacrifice (variable); Christmas (December 25/26); Revolution Day (December 31)

TIME LINE

IN GHANA	IN THE WORLD
5500–2500 B.C. Hunter-gatherer communities formed in plains around Ghana.	
	A.D. 600 Height of Mayan civilization.
A.D. 1200 The Akan people's kingdom grows in Ghana's northern grasslands.	**1206–1368** Genghis Khan unifies the Mongols and starts conquest of the wor[ld]. At its height, the Mongol Empire under Kublai Khan stretches fro[m] China to Persia and parts of Europe and Russia.
1471 Portuguese traders arrive near Elmina.	
1481 Portuguese mission led by Diogo d'Azambuja discovers gold in Volta plains.	
1482 Portuguese build castle at Elmina to enhance trading in gold and slaves.	**1492** Christopher Columbus sets foot in America.
1500 The Ga and Adangme tribes settle around Accra.	**1506** Portuguese control east Ghanian coast.
1598 The Dutch build forts along Ghana's coastal area to secure trade.	
1600 The Ewe people from Benin settle in Ghana.	
1637 The Dutch capture Portuguese forts.	
1650 The English, Germans, and Danes build forts in Ghana.	
1674 Britain makes the Gold Coast a crown colony.	
1662 Britain establishes headquarters at Cape Coast Castle.	**1776** U.S. Declaration of Independence.
1925 First legislative council elections take place.	**1939** World War II begins.
1947 First political party, United Gold Coast Convention (UGCC) forms.	
1949 Kwame Nkrumah forms the Convention People's Party (CPP).	**1949** The North Atlantic Treaty Organization (NATO) is formed.
1952 Kwame Nkrumah is designated prime minister of the British colony's first African government.	**1950–53** The Korean War between North and South Korea.
1957 Ghana, with Kwame Nkrumah as prime minister, becomes the first African country to be granted independence.	**1957** The Russians launch Sputnik.

IN GHANA	IN THE WORLD
1960	
Ghana is proclaimed a republic. Dr. Kwame Nkrumah is elected president of Ghana.	
1964	
Ghana becomes a one-party state.	
1966	**1966**
Nkrumah is ousted in a military coup.	The Chinese Cultural Revolution.
1969	**1969**
New constitution facilitates transfer of power to civilian government led by Kofi Busia.	*Apollo 11* lands the first men on the moon.
1972	
Busia is overthrown in a military coup led by Colonel Ignatius Acheampong.	**1975**
1978	Khmer Rouge ruthlessly rules Cambodia, led by despot Pol Pot.
Acheampong is forced to resign. General Frederick Akuffo takes over.	
1979	
Akuffo is deposed in coup led by Flight Lieutenant Jerry Rawlings. Achaempong and Akuffo are executed on charges of corruption. Rawlings hands over power to an elected president, Hilla Limann.	
1981	
Limann ousted in military coup led by Rawlings.	**1991**
1992	Breakup of the Soviet Union.
Rawlings elected president. New constitution introduces a multiparty system.	
1994	
Ethnic clashes in Northern Region between the Konkomba and the Nanumba.	
1996	
Jerry Rawlings reelected president.	
2001	**2001**
John Agyekum Kufour is elected president. Serves until 2009.	Arab terrorists crash planes in New York, Washington D.C. and Pennsylvania, September 11.
2002	
President Kufour appoints reconciliation commission to look into human rights violations during military rule.	**2003**
2005	War in Iraq begins.
Thousands of Togolese refugees fleeing political violence arrive in Ghana.	
2007	
Ghana celebrates 50 years independence.	
2008	
Professor John Evans Atta Mills is elected president.	

GLOSSARY

abosom (ah-BOH-som)
Akan name for an animist spirit.

abusa (ah-BOO-sah)
Clan or family grouping.

adae (AHD-ay)
A period of 40 days in the Akan calendar.

akpeteshe (ak-pet-ESH-ee)
Distilled palm wine.

akwaba (ak-WAH-bah)
Welcome.

amanee (ah-MAH-nee)
Custom of asking and explaining reasons for a home visit.

apaat (ap-AHT)
A game similar to cricket.

apirede (ap-eer-EH-deh
A traditional orchestral ensemble consisting of drums, a gong, and clappers, played by ceremonial Ashanti stool carriers.

atumpan (at-UM-pan)
Talking drum of the Akan.

bogya (BOG-yah)
Physical aspect of a human being.

durbar
Pageant during a festival.

enstoolment
The ceremony of enthroning a new chief.

fetish house
A building dedicated to an animist spirit.

fufu (FOO-foo)
A staple food made from pounded cassava and either plantain or cocoyam.

highlife
African big band music.

juju
A form of folk medicine practiced by animist priests.

kente cloth
Traditional Ashanti cloth, woven in colorful strips, sewn together to make clothing.

malam
A Muslim religious healer in Ghana.

nton (n-TON)
The spiritual aspect of being.

okyeame (otch-ee-AH-mee)
Linguist who accompanies the chief.

oware (oh-WAR-eh)
Traditional variant of mancala, somewhat like backgammon, played on the ground with seeds or pebbles.

pito (PEE-toh)
A beer brewed from millet.

tro tro (TRO tro)
A van that functions as a taxi in towns; called a mammy wagon in the countryside.

FOR FURTHER INFORMATION

BOOKS

Amamoo, Joseph. *The New Ghana: The Birth of a Nation*. India: iUniverse, 2000.

Briggs, Philip. *Ghana*, 4th edition (Bradt Travel Guides). Guilford, CT: The Globe Pequot Press, 2007.

Milne, June. *Kwame Nkrumah: A Biography*. United Kingdom: Panaf Books, 2000.

Randall, Peter E., and Abena Busia. *Ghana: An African Portrait Revisited*. Portsmouth, NH: Peter E. Randall Publisher, 2007.

FILMS

Wendl, Tobias, and Nancy du Plessis. *The Art of Remembering: Photography, Art and Anthropology in Ghana*, 1998.

MUSIC

Asante Kete Drumming: Music of Ghana, Lyrichord Discs Inc., 2007.

Black Stars: Ghana's Hiplife Generation, Out Here Records, 2008.

Ewe Drumming from Ghana, Topic Records, 2005.

Ghana: Rhythms of the People, Music Earth, 2000.

Por Por: Honk Horn Music of Ghana, Smithsonian Folkways, 2007.

BIBLIOGRAPHY

BOOKS

Africa. Oakland, CA: Lonely Planet Publications, 1995.

Brace, Steve. *Ghana* (Economically Developing Countries). Hove, UK: Wayland (Publishers), 1994.

Edgerton, Robert B. *The Fall of the Asante Empire: The Hundred-Year War for Africa's Gold Coast.* New York: The Free Press, 1995.

Hadjor, Kofi Buenor. *Nkrumah and Ghana.* London: Kegan Paul International, 1988.

Ray, Donald Iain. *Ghana: Politics, Economics, and Society* (Marxist Regimes Series). Boulder, CO: L. Rienner Publishers, 1986.

Trillo, Richard and Jim Hudgens. *The Rough Guide to West Africa.* New York: The Rough Guides Publisher, 2009.

WEBSITES

Central Intelligence Agency World Factbook (select Ghana from country list). www.cia.gov/cia/publications/factbook/index.html

Food in Ghana. www.foodbycountry.com/Germany-to-Japan/Ghana.html

Ghana Home Page. www.ghanaweb.com/GhanaHomePage/sitemap.php

Ghana Official Portal. www.ghana.gov.gh/the_executive

Ghana tourism home page. www.touringghana.com/

National Geographic Magazine: High-Tech Trash. http://ngm.nationalgeographic.com/print/2008/01/high-tech-trash/carroll-text

Moving up from Akosombo. http://waterpowermagazine.com/story.asp?storyCode=2049535

INDEX

INDEX